INTERVIEW WITH THE BOOGEYMAN

A MONSTER FOR ALL TIMES

BENJAMIN S. JEFFRIES

Schiffer Publishing Ltd

4880 Lower Valley Road • Atglen, PA 19310

DEDICATION

For my father,
Arliss Jeffries.
The best storyteller I ever knew,
and the greatest father there ever will be.
(Even though he'll likely call me out for ending that phrase with a verb.)

"So, I think he knew on that bright morning, that he'd made a memory
that would live as long as sons tell sons about fathers they love."
—Ray Bradbury
Something Wicked This Way Comes

Copyright © 2017 by Benjamin S. Jeffries

Library of Congress Control Number: 2017936138

Ouija is a registered trademark of Hasbro.
Twinkies is a registered trademark of Hostess

Cover & Interior designed by Matthew Goodman
Type set in Cochin, Nicolas Cochin EF & DeRoss

ISBN: 978-0-7643-5307-9

Printed in China

Published by Schiffer Publishing, Ltd.
4880 Lower Valley Road
Atglen, PA 19310
Phone: (610) 593-1777;
Fax: (610) 593-2002
E-mail: Info@schifferbooks.com
Web: www.schifferbooks.com

For our complete selection of fine books on this and related subjects, please visit our website at www.schifferbooks.com. You may also write for a free catalog.

Schiffer Publishing's titles are available at special discounts for bulk purchases for sales promotions or premiums. Special editions, including personalized covers, corporate imprints, and excerpts, can be created in large quantities for special needs. For more information, contact the publisher.

We are always looking for people to write books on new and related subjects. If you have an idea for a book, please contact us at proposals@schifferbooks.com.

**Other Schiffer Books
by Benjamin S. Jeffries:**

Grim Shadows Falling:
Haunting Tales from
Terrifying Places.
ISBN: 978-0-7643-4708-5

Lost in the Darkness:
Life Inside the World's Most Haunted Prisons,
Hospitals, and Asylums.
ISBN: 978-0-7643-4319-3

Vile—
Peeking Under the Skin
of Murderers.
ISBN: 978-0-7643-5090-0

**Other Schiffer Books
on Related Subjects:**

Haunted Closets:
True Tales of The Boogeyman.
Katie Boyd.
ISBN: 978-0-7643-3474-0

I. Lucifer:
Exploring the Archetype
and Origins of the Devil.
Corvis Nocturnum.
ISBN: 978-0-7643-3919-6

Under Spiritual Siege:
How Ghosts and Demons Affect Us
and How to Combat Them.
William Stillman.
ISBN: 978-0-7643-5042-9

Devils and Demonology:
In the 21st Century.
Katie Boyd.
ISBN: 978-0-7643-3195-4

CONTENTS

INTRODUCTION

THE TRUE FACE OF FEAR

A T THE TIME, I was on a mission for a completely different book than this one. I wasn't cheating on this book; I was just scouting some old farmhouses that resembled Ed Gein's old farmhouse for my previous book, *VILE: Peeking Under the Skin of Murderers*. Since Ed's old place burned down in the 1950s, finding a turn-of-the-century farmhouse that looked like his was a daunting task, especially in a town notorious for tearing down the old, effectively erasing history rather than risk renovation and preserving the past.

It was a few miles outside of Frankfort, Indiana. Almost two hours had passed and I was intent on heading home when I felt a sudden pull, kind of like when you feel you're being watched and you have to stop everything you're doing to acknowledge that person watching you. I pulled to a halt and saw the house immediately. I'd driven down this road at least three times already, but I never noticed the old place before, hidden by overgrown foliage and trees. A window and the beginning of an old brick wall were all I could see from the road. A narrow drive guarded by low hanging branches crept into view and I pulled in. The arms of the trees, the disappearance of the sun, and the tingling ball of agitating energy in my guts began bouncing back and forth. I stopped my truck and got out.

It was a three-story farmhouse, like one I had been looking for, and I cradled my camera in my hands as I looked for signs of life on the property. No other vehicles save for a broken-down old tractor, engulfed by the woods and weeds, were in sight. It had all the feel of a graveyard.

It was a solid red-brick monstrosity. White paint on the trim and porches had yellowed in spots and was starting to crack and peel away from the wood. Windows were cracked in places, and all of them looked to be coated in a thin layer of age. The front door hung open, slung low on only one hinge. A barn to the left and near the back of the house looked like it was about to fall in upon itself. Trees and brush were everywhere, but I heard no birds singing, no insects chirping. It even seemed as if the wind refused to blow through there, and the sun had no power over what was here; even though it was obviously daytime, the sun now hid behind clouds and refused to brighten this blight any further.

The lawn was overgrown with knee-high grass that hid an old tricycle, a sandbox, some old Tonka trucks. A pump well looked like it had been rusted shut for years.

There was a voice in my ear, soft and almost non-existent: "Here," it said, so softly. I turned toward the front door. Darkness filled the inside of the house and I heard it again.

"Here..."

A voice soft as silk—but filled with gravel and dark intentions. As terrifying a voice as it was seductive, it reached into me with a gaseous hand and pulled at my guts and spine, leaving goose flesh in its wake, and without realizing it, I was standing in the doorway.

"In..."

All the way in the back, down what must have been a hallway leading to the kitchen, was a window that let in light, but it never traveled beyond the perimeter of the glass, looking much like a light box used in those artsy graphic design places. And it was through that light that I saw the shadow move, from right to left, slowly. It had no form other than the wispy blackness it was made of, and if it were the head of something, I watched it turn and look on me as it moved.

"In..."

I ignored the dark and all the insecurity it held and walked toward the light. I noticed the rotting floor creaking and bowing beneath my feet, but I didn't fret over it. I was aware of a staircase to my right, a solid wall of old pictures to my left, and the light in front of me grew brighter and larger as I got closer.

As I stood in the kitchen, a movement to the left caught my eye.

It stood in the doorway leading to the basement, tall and gaseous, black and smoky with two bright white eyes that seeped into my heart as its spindly fingers motioned for me.

"Follow..."

And it was gone, down the stairs and into the cellar. I froze. I couldn't move, my fear was binding me to the spot, and I began to wish I'd brought a flashlight instead of my camera.

"Down..."

Even as I resolved to stay where I was, it felt as if the thing in the cellar had taken hold of my hand and was pulling me toward the darkness beyond. The closer I got to the doorway, the more my fear intensified. Walking down the steep, rickety steps, I could immediately smell the moist scent of stale air and layers of dust that most basements hold. And even though I was walking toward an uncertain fate, I had no reservations, as if I was meant to be in this position. Standing at the foot of the stairs, I saw the outlines of what must have been a newer model furnace, washer, and dryer. While odd that such new utilities could be found in such an old, abandoned home, the Thing in the basement distracted me completely.

It was now standing in the doorway of the old coal room, waving me over with its smoky hand before becoming one with the darkness again.

"Follow..."

I did as I was told, stepping into the small room as I felt around for walls and a light switch. Its voice came out all around me, still a bit gravely, but not nearly as ethereal or ghostly. It was as if it were in the room with me.

"No lights, at least not yet," said the Thing. "But in time."

"Who are you?" I asked.

"It is not a matter of 'who' but of 'what', and you know what I am, your mind just has trouble accepting it." A pause. "We have met before, you and I, though I believe you may have been too young to remember. It *was* forty years ago, after all."

"What do you want?"

I could feel It move around me, Its voice moving from one ear to another before I heard It again in both. "Your fear is stronger within you than you are willing to admit, boy. That's why I chose you. You are still frightened by those things in the dark that shouldn't be there. You understand it more than others might, yet it still frightens you. You want to be a part of the darkness, but you're scared of it and what it may bring. I am here to bring that fear out of you and to give you the opportunity to tell a tale that no one has ever written of or heard before. Are you interested?"

"What are you? What do I call you?"

I heard the scoot of wood on concrete, and the light, tingly pressing of the Things hand on my chest as it gently pushed me into the chair it had pulled up for me.

"I met you in the winter of 1975," it began. "You had just turned four. At the time, you knew me as a beast in the dark, but in the light, I was nothing more than the bathrobe you left strewn on that old rocking chair.

From your closet door, I watched you and I saw my influence grow on you. Monsters, madmen, creatures, and horror . . . it all came from the Thing in the closet who terrified you each night."

"The Boogeyman," I whispered.

"I have had many names over the years. For thousands of years I have lived upon the fright of youth and the terrors trapped in the pensive night. I chose you, boy, to write my tale, my saga. Many lives have I lived and each one throbs with a heartbeat that is longing to be heard. So many sights to show and tales to tell."

"Why me?"

"Well, you weren't my first choice. Stephen King and Clive Barker wouldn't go anywhere or do anything without their agents. Same thing went for Bradbury when he was alive. But in all honesty, no one else made it past the front door but you. So . . . you win by default."

I scoffed a little and smirked in the dark. "Thanks."

"Don't let it bother you. You did better than Bret Easton Ellis, who I love, and that guy who writes for *Creepypasta* . . . Ricardo-something. But you understand: if you can get King or Barker to write your life story, wouldn't you try that first?"

The Thing had a point.

"Beneath your chair you'll find a leather-bound book. Many loose pages, some of which are very old, so be careful when you go through it. Read it, use it to form the basis of your work, and when you're through with it, I will be here to fill in any blanks you might have."

I felt around and, indeed, found a large leathery book on the floor beneath my seat. It was tied end-to-end with a thick piece of cowhide string, keeping its contents from falling out. "What is it?"

"A journal of my work." His voice was wistful, proud. I felt the smooth leather in the darkness and I felt the cold touch of his wispy fingers as they traced across the embroidered cover. It was as if he were bidding farewell to an old friend. "Do you agree?" he asked again.

I nodded in the dark, punctuating it with a very emphatic response. "Yes, yes I do."

"Excellent," he replied with elation. "Now that we hold a covenant between each other, perhaps it is best that I introduce myself properly."

The coal room was suddenly flooded with light. My eyes slammed shut, and even when I opened them, there was a gauzy aura around everything. But I could still see the wispy hand come away from the pull-chain of the light fixture that dangled overhead, and as I followed the hand, I found myself staring into the same white eyes of the creature I'd seen upstairs.

It was essentially a man formed of black smoke, and when it moved, it left dusky vapor trails in its wake that dissipated into the thickening air. The Thing's eyes were blinding white, looking more like tiny balls of light than actual eyes. No other feature was evident, not even a mouth or nose.

"I am Tenebris," it said. "And we have quite a journey ahead of us, boy. Are you ready?"

I'd never been more certain of anything in my life, up until this point. I opened the journal. Immediately, I looked to Tenebris. "Latin?"

Though it had no visible mouth, I could swear it was smiling. When I left the house, when I got into my truck, and even when I was mere seconds from walking in my front door, I knew I wasn't alone. It was in the journal beside me and it had slid into my soul. In my heart, I felt the cool touch of its presence and when I slept at night, I slept knowing its eye was fixed upon me.

It took me five weeks to transcribe the Latin text into Google Translate. As beautiful as Google is, their translation software left a lot of cracks in the English translation. Some phrases were backwards, some weren't even able to be translated.

But it made no difference. By the time I got to page three, I was reading it perfectly, cracks, gaps, and all. Amazing how the brain works. But I barely made it through all those pages when I just had to stop. It was too much. How was this even possible? I was reading from the handwritten diary of a mythological creature who seemed to have a great sense of humor and a tremendously insightful memory of how things worked in this old, dark world of myth and fable. But here it was. In black and white, sometimes in red. The life story of the boogeyman, sprung to life on pages a thousand years old, in ink poured from its own gaseous hand.

In time, most of us have met this marvel of darkness, this shape-shifting creature of timeless wonder. To some, it became a pile of clothes in our bedrooms, or a shadow on the wall that couldn't possibly have been the reflection of a skeletal tree branch in the moonlight. For me, the boogeyman was the thing in the closet with two shiny eyes peering out at me from the cracked open t door. Its camouflage was flawless, blending into the darkness and making it seem as if its eyes were nothing but two polished coat buttons reflecting light in the dark.

But I knew it was there. It was *always* there. It's there still. Only now, in the throes of depressing adulthood, real life terrors have replaced the made up ones that only children can concoct. To us now, as adults, it oftentimes seems fun and cute. But I don't remember the monsters being fun or cute. I remember them as being absolutely terrifying, and only a good blanket stitched together by your mother's saintly fingers could protect you from the monstrosity. This is how blanket forts came to be, by the way. An imaginative kid with a decent-sized blanket could fit a radio, three books (or twelve comic books), two flashlights (in case one ran out of batteries), half a box of Twinkies, and four grape sodas into his blanket fort, which could also be described as an Anti-Boogey Fortress. You had to have provisions, you know—just in case the boogeyman was patient that night and tried to wait you out until dawn. And once you were under that blanket, you were safe. You might have heard a shuffling around the room as he circled your bed, or maybe heard his heavy breathing as he got as close to the blanket as he could without touching it, but you were safe.

What's more frightening is the fact that the boogeyman didn't just visit us every night. He would visit all of our friends, too. And their friends. And all of *their* friends. And all around the world, Tenebris, The Boogeyman would appear in different countries, becoming fixtures in different cultures, the villain in different legends. He was a moral crusader who doled out punishment to naughty children in ways that could make your stomach do jumping jacks.

So, what is it about the boogeyman that frightens even the most jaded writers, paranormal investigators, and horror film fans? Could it be its mysterious origin of which we know very little? Or perhaps it is its uncanny ability to use the darkness of our own sanctuary—our bedrooms—to hide its true form and intention? It is every nightmare you've ever had and every fear made flesh. It is the most feared villain in the history of the world, haunting us past childhood, lingering in the background of the darkest recesses of our souls. It is the reason why we don't dangle our feet over the side of the bed and why we fear the night. Evil despots, terrorists, and Biblical creatures, such as Adolph Hitler, Osama Bin Laden, and The Devil cannot even compare to It, for you could *possibly* reason with them, even talk terms with them. But *no one* can negotiate with the boogeyman. No one dares even speak its name aloud for fear that this will summon it.

As the years labor on, its form has changed to reflect the times, and in the face of the jaded new millennium, it is seen as a far more disturbing, bloodthirsty, and unforgiving creature that will abduct the souls of children and leave behind wounds that will never heal on the souls of their family and friends.

The true story of the boogeyman began when recorded time was merely a toddler and the earliest known ancestors of man had recently begun life out of trees. It came into being on a dark day in what would be the month of May in the northern part of Iceland amid a rough hewn mountain range formed from bubbling lava fields and multitudes of active volcanoes. Once the lava cooled and the flows ceased, the chimneys of the volcanoes and parts of the thick black lava rock remained. These naturally formed mountains resembled eerie towers, walls, and gates. Local villagers, superstitious even to this day, saw the darkness in that place, saw the potential for evil in its unusual rock formations, and dubbed the region the Dimmuborgir, which was Icelandic for "Dark Town." Many believed that this forbidding place was where Lucifer himself landed when he was cast from Heaven by God.

The being that emerged from the ash, rock, and vapor of Dimmuborgir knew its intent and purpose from the beginning, leading one to believe that Tenebris was born out of pure fear itself. Fear, as we all know, is an innate, primal feeling that we seem to be born with, and with that fear comes its inevitable personifications. For Cro-Magnon and Neanderthal man, the fears they suffered came in the form of vicious animal attacks and life-changing weather events, such as earthquakes, typhoons, and debilitating blizzards. Still, these were things that they could partially anticipate and prepare for as part of their lives.

But there were some things that they couldn't readily explain, things not easily understood. One of these things was how fire came to be, that mysterious element of heat that hurt like a sonofabitch but somehow made food taste better. While the presence of fire brightened the caves and cooked their meat, it also created the deepest, darkest shadows that danced in their peripheral vision. With the addition of flame and shadow came the explanations for which early man had been searching. Shadows became ghosts, the vengeful spirits of slain enemies. Lightning flung to earth had been hurled onto them by mischievous creatures. It was from this darkness that the creature we know as The Boogeyman rose to prominence, fed by fear and made whole by wandering imaginations. It became more than aware of Its surroundings early on, first by manipulating the shadows from which it had been born and then by evolving into the shape-shifting beast it is now famous for. As fear of the dark proliferated, the presence of the boogeyman did as well, casting Its spidery arms and spreading his primal fear across the world, infecting cave systems and cultures with its anthropomorphic creativity.

But somewhere along the line, Tenebris went from being a harmless shade in the dark to being an absolute fearsome creature that could—and would—reach out and take what it wanted. Children began disappearing from their beds in the dead of night, taken to a land of eternal night as a punishment for misbehaving or, in some rare cases, as retribution for their parents' misdeeds.

When I finally met with The Boogeyman for this book, it was excited to finally get its own story straight for those generations of people who

The old house as seen from the road. (*Photo by author.*)

had maligned it. Admittedly, it did come clean and claim responsibility for terrorizing literally billions of people in its time, but was adamant: they had it coming, calling his job "an offshoot of the Fates, working in the same office of ironic punishments as Santa Claus, the Easter Bunny, and Dick Cheney."

That, unfortunately, was as much information as he was willing to divulge at first, though he did read the final draft and made several valid suggestions. He would become more comfortable with me and I with him, and it really made for a very cool, very switched-on collaboration. "It" became a "he" and the "creature" became "Tenebris." Born in darkness, we became as familiar with each other as brothers might. He's also a lot funnier than I would have thought a Boogeyman should (or could) be. In the end, I think I was able to divine his exploits from literally thousands of years of history, which, in my eyes, made for a fairly good look at the true face of fear.

PRELIMINARY INTERVIEW

TENEBRIS, THE BOOGEYMAN

Location: Clinton County, Abandoned Farm House Basement Coal Room

Date: October 12, 2015

How did you happen to come into being?

I was born of shadow and fear. Long ago when slime walked out of the ocean and became mammalian carnivores on two legs, an evolution began. With that evolution came knowledge, thought, and artistic expression. But along with those glorious traits of evolution also came fear, paranoia, and curiosity. Just as man evolved from the lowest of the low, I did as well, snatching their fear and using it to feed. From the shadows I came and from the shadows I grew, always on the outside, always looking in. I was born of the shadow, but I was fathered by mankind, so I could always see into them very easily. Just as I saw the love they had for one another, I could also see their fears; each one was specific to the individual.

I first saw the light of the sun in what is now known as Iceland, in the heart of the Dimmuborgir Lava Fields, a region that I will speak about later. It was the indigenous cave people, Cro-Magnon, and later, Homo-erectus, who gave me a true sense of life. It was their misunderstanding of the world in which they lived that gave my pulse its purpose, and my breath, its lightning. I was the shadow on the cave wall, the beast in the forest at night. The thing below the frozen seas and rivers.

Over time and throughout history, I too evolved into what I am now.

What is your favorite memory of those early years?

My friendship with Satan, God, and Plato. We all go way back. Plato was only there because he was able to reason with God and win a spot at the card table. We used to call him "New Guy." He hated that.

I was with Satan one day, who'd just been reassigned to the Underworld because he had a knack for ironic punishments that God was too skittish to dole out after his Son was born. Fatherhood changed him, I tell you. Just read the Old Testament. Multitudinous stories of fire, blood, vengeance, and almost cruel punishments. But in the New Testament, where Jesus makes his first appearance? He's become a very mellow, almost complacent deity with an emphasis on love. Tell me being a father didn't affect him.

It was I who tempted Eve in the garden that first time. Satan challenged me that I could not get her to stray from God's word. I had already convinced Lilith that Adam was cheating on her, despite the fact that they were the only two in the garden. Oh, was she mad. Got herself expelled very quickly. So I took up the "Eve Challenge" without a second thought. The rest is history. Satan mostly takes credit for it now, though I still use the snake in my work more than any other creature.

Here's an interesting tidbit: God and Satan . . . they worked out the whole universe themselves. They weren't "best buddies" per se, but God saw the need for a consequence to those who had lived badly. He didn't want them in Heaven, and he didn't want them walking the earth as spirits cut loose into the cosmos. So Hell was created, though in those days it was known as "Ignis Insula" before the term "Hell" was stolen from a much older, more refined folktale of the Nordic underworld.

So God and the Devil are in cahoots?

It's a tenuous relationship. They don't talk like they used to, but its very much a symbiotic kinship that they have. I haven't spoken to either of them in so long that I really can't say how they are doing now. But what I do know is that there is no reason why Hell should be as full as it is. People are wrong to hate the Devil. They should *fear* the Devil. The path to Hell is lined with the hatred of its occupants. Hatred is what takes you to Hell. It's why Hitler and Bin Laden burn there now. Fear, like I've said, breeds strength to overcome it. So if more people were afraid of the consequences of their actions, and consider them more often, then Hell would be as quiet and as empty as one of your book signings.

Ouch. Speaking of Hitler and Bin Laden, most people refer to them as "boogeymen." Are you proud or insulted?

Insulted, to say the least. They were horrible people who preyed on fear, true, but they do so to recreate the world to suit them. I, on the other hand, use my gift for fear to empower and strengthen those who are weaker.

Seriously?

My exploits are tales of morality with a lesson to be learned in each scenario. Those who learn why they fear eventually conquer their fear. They are free of it. Forever.

Hitler and Bin Laden? They only sought to destroy their fear by erasing it from around them, not from within them. Even when they died, their fear lived on, picked up by sheep who continued their misguided fight to destroy their own innate fear by shedding innocent blood. That makes them weaker than the five-year-old children who are able to learn from and conquer their fear.

Many of your incarnations target children. Is there a reason for that other than the obvious answer of attempting to get mischievous children to behave?

There are tales of how I terrify children and I have done that for thousands of years. By terrifying the child, I also terrify the parent, though in recent years, I've seen many parents attempting to collude with me to get their children to behave, which I don't necessarily agree with, but I do what I have to do to get my nut out of the tree.

I'm not here to do the job of the parents, but they often force my hand by painting a rather lurid picture of me before I even stick one hand out from under the bed. I live on fear, and when they conquer the Boggarts I send them, I move on. In many ways, some parents are worse boogey-men than I. The scariest ones are the ones who live off the fear of their own children instead of trying to help them conquer it. Many a mother and father have I encountered who are this way. It's sad, but its also aggravating. It takes the desperation out of fear and removes the emphatic joy from a hard-fought victory.

Speaking of your various incarnations, do you have a favorite? And do you have a least-favorite?

I always had a soft spot for Grendel. Hated Beowulf, but Grendel was always a favorite.

As for my least favorite? The Bunny-man hands down. Remember that scene in *A Christmas Story* where Ralphie puts on the pink bunny costume? That's *exactly* how I felt every time I had to appear as the Bunny-man. So glad that one passed from the collective conscious.

Which do you prefer: the closet or under the bed? Why?
Under the bed. It's just so much more personal. I can hear their heart rates increase, feel the bed tremble as they shake in terror. Plus, when you're under the bed, the kiddies will never see you coming.

The only drawback are the ones who are occupied by bed-wetters.

Another good one is underneath the stairs. I've gotten quite a few that way. They never expect that hand to come out and grab their ankles. And there's usually no blankets.

Biggest pet peeve?
Children who make blanket forts. Worst. Kept. Secret. Ever. Seriously, if I find the kid who spread the word that I can't get past a child's blanket, we will exchange more than just words. Not that it's a total loss. It only makes the chase more interesting. Always nice to be kept on my toes.

Why is that?
Most children's first blankets are not made by Walmart; they are made by their mother's laborious fingertips. Or grandmother's. Nothing in the world is more powerful than a mother's love for her children, and it all goes into their first blanket. (*Pause*) I probably shouldn't have told you that.

Favorite big screen depiction of you?
Bughuul from *Sinister* was a good one.

What is something people would be surprised to learn about you?
I once attended college classes with Alexander Haig at Columbia. I learned a lot from him about instilling fear and making it grow, and I think he learned just as much from me as well. Our track records speak for themselves, though he was much more interested in gaining power than I was.

Biggest rumor you'd like to squelch right now?
That I started Creepypasta. Love their work, but they took that ball and ran with it without my help. Good for them!

Favorite type of music?

I've always preferred classical, especially Prokofiev. His work was just fun, full of life! But I must say that I love Dimmu Borgir and Amon Amarth as well. Great Nordic heavy metal with that prominent classical influence. Reminds me of home.

You seem to have a terrific sense of humor.

It can't rain all the time. Even a boogeyman needs to smile sometimes. Some would argue that a smiling boogeyman is creepier anyway.

"SOMETHING WAS CREEPING AND CREEPING AND WAITING TO BE SEEN AND FELT AND HEARD."

—H.P. Lovecraft, *The Colour of Space*

CHAPTER ONE

BLOOD UPON THE ICE

THE TERROR OF SCANDINAVIA

FROM DEEP WITHIN the Dimmuborgir Lava Fields, I rose from the fires and molten rock to breed fear. This land, this dark world of Scandinavia, would be the first to feel my icy fingers on their necks as they rode their carriages and horses home. Home: they thought they were safe there. But the itching of fear under their skin multiplied when they realized that they had led me to their safe havens and that there was no defense against the horror I had planned for them all. In time, the darkest parts of their hearts and homes would be breeding grounds for my legend, and I would spread my wings in time, casting a shroud of gloom across the world. The Scandinavian dark bred monsters with ease and I filled the void left by the ascension of Odin and his gods. When man became too confident within the dark, I came to remind them of the way things truly are when the moon rises and the imagination swirls with contemplation.

—From the diary of Tenebris, The Boogeyman

BEOWULF AND GRENDEL

TENEBRIS CAME INTO prominence quickly when he took on the role of what is now considered folklore's greatest villain, but while many dismiss Grendel as the wild imaginings of an anonymous poet, he is quick to point out that both Beowulf and Grendel were as real as the blood inside of my veins, though the actions in the poem differ slightly from the reality, such as the reality that Beowulf was only four feet eight inches tall and that Grendel's arm separated from his body only when he turned wrong and got caught in the Mead Hall door. It was this unfortunate accident that prompted the dwarf-like Beowulf to claim his fraudulent victory over Grendel.

> Beowulf obviously had some insecurities to overcome, not including his diminutive size, for what kind of man seeks out danger if he has nothing to prove to himself? My time as Grendel was short lived, and he certainly wasn't the first I'd become, but the experience changed how I conducted everything, most definitely. He became the blueprint for all others that came after.
>
> — From the diary of Tenebris, The Boogeyman

While the story of Beowulf and Grendel is an old English tale, its characters and locations are cemented firmly in the lands of Scandinavia, most prominently the kingdom of Denmark, and while it was first recorded by an Englishman, it began as a story told around Norse fires, camps, and mead halls, concocted by Vikings and spread about so much that it reached the darkest corners of the Earth before being immortalized around 700 AD. Written to laud the exploits of its main character, *Beowulf* would become more known for its monsters, namely the fearsome and terrifying Grendel.

The story tells of a heroic Norseman named Beowulf and his small band of mercenaries, brutish men who desired not power or fortune, but glory and legend. Beowulf and his companions would find that and more when they entered the kingdom of Hrothgar, king of the Danes. Hrothgar was a king with a dark and gruesome problem, one that was hideous, monstrous, and unrelenting. For years, the beastly creature Grendel had struck out at Hrothgar's men, dismembering them with his bare hands and painting the king's mead hall red with their blood. But it never touched Hrothgar, for the king protected himself by sitting upon a throne blessed and dedicated to the gods. As long as Hrothgar sat on this throne, Grendel could not touch him. In doing so, Grendel forced King Hrothgar to watch as he massacred his most decorated soldiers.

Beowulf was a warrior from the south, a region known as Geatland, which was a rugged city near the coast line. He was neither royal nor rich, but had a taste for high adventure and eagerly sought to make a name for himself. When he heard of Hrothgar's plight, he and his men took off for the king's land, vowing to do what no one else could do: slay Grendel. Setting a trap for the beast by staging a raucous party, Beowulf and his men lay in wait of Grendel, who did not disappoint. Several of

Beowulf's men were destroyed before Beowulf himself wrenched Grendel's massive arm off and sent the howling man-beast in the woods where he bled to death in the darkness.

But with the death of Grendel came the wrath of his mother, who sought out Beowulf with a vengeance. She attacked Hrothgar's Mead Hall and slew Hrothgar's most trusted adviser, AEschere, knowing it would bring Beowulf to her. Her plan worked and Beowulf and his men set out for the swamplands to meet her. Grendel's mother lived under the water in a secret lair that was accessible only to the strongest men who could survive the dive. Diving into the murky water, Beowulf swam deeply into the swamp water and soon came upon the lair. It is here that Beowulf fights, and slays, Grendel's mother, destroying her

The first page of the original *Beowulf* manuscript, c. 700 AD. (*Artist unknown.*)

with a sword originally forged for a Frost Giant. Recovering Grendel's corpse, Beowulf took the head and returned to Hrothgar's palace. He would go on to return to Geatland, where he would slay the third monster in the story, a fearsome dragon.

With the story of Beowulf, we have a pretty good idea of where the story of the boogeyman really began. In almost every aspect, Grendel can be seen as the template for just about every incarnation of the boogeyman that would ever come to be. He struck at night, he was nearly indestructible, and he was a loathsome, beastly creature that seemed to abhor anything that was good and decent. Thought to be written around 700 AD, the story of Beowulf and Grendel could very well have been tossed around campfires for hundreds of years before someone thought to write it down. Though there were monsters before Grendel, when put into that context, it is easy to see how he could inspire the multitude of boogeymen that would follow in the years to come.

The story of Beowulf's heroics were told in such bland and generic terms that varying interpretations of the tale came almost immediately. Storytellers of the time felt a need to fill in the holes with pertinent information to make the story better rounded, while historians and literature enthusiasts of late filled in the holes with archaic and logical facts in an effort to make it more authentic.

"However you choose to interpret Beowulf, there's no denying that it's one of the greatest adventure stories of all time," writes C. Hollis Crossman, a critic at ExodusBooks.com. "Reading it simply on this level is no injustice, since it was primarily intended to entertain tired warriors in some dark mead hall in Daneland. While the Anglo-Saxon blood has long since faded, the nostalgia their greatest poem produces never will."

When looked upon at face value, Grendel is nothing more than a one-dimensional monster. But peering deeper into what possibly drives him, such as the obvious rage that controls him, one can easily see what makes Grendel work as a Boogeyman. His general nature isn't all monstrous. Though his appearance is vile and his actions are brutal, he's a creature driven by human emotions, impulses, and reactions. His rage at being exiled is understandable and he seems to long to be accepted once more. He's driven by loneliness and lives through his jealousy of those who have things that he wants. As sympathetic as people may want Grendel to seem, the original text brands Grendel irredeemable, describing him as being of "Cain's clan, whom the creator had outlawed/and condemned as outcasts." He is further described as "[m]alignant by nature" and that he has "never show[n] remorse." It is a common, internal struggle that would lead the way for characters such as Darth Vader, Frankenstein's Monster, and the Golem: once irredeemable villains who harbor a secret hurt in the darkest parts of their souls that will ultimately lead them up to the light.

THE BOOGG

EVERY YEAR IN the Swiss city of Zurich, the spring holiday of Sechseläuten is celebrated. Literally translated, *Sechseläuten* means "the six o'clock ringing of the bells" and commemorates the beginning of Spring, when the days are longer and the nights are shorter. Similar to the Celtic festival of Samhain, Sechseläuten boasts its own fearsome mascot of the celebration, one who pays the ultimate price at the conclusion.

At the climax of the Sechseläuten is the traditional "Burning of The Boogg," in which a flammable, 100-foot statue of a snowman is lit aflame and burned. The Boogg (pronounced "Bok") is a symbol going back to medieval times that represented winter and death, and while the Boogg of today may seem cartoonish, amiable, and even cuddly, his legend rises from a nasty, scary boogeyman who first appeared in the earliest days of Switzerland's dark folklore.

The original Boogg was a hooded creature in black, stalking the dark, stone streets of Zurich, peering into the bedroom windows of children.

Other tales placed him under their beds at night or lurking behind closet doors. Obviously the precursor to the more popular Boogeyman, the Boogg struck during the winter months when nights were longer and darker than normal.

Stories of the Boogg vary from region to region, as do descriptions of him. But most agree that the Boogg is seen as standing over seven feet tall, swathed in thick black robes, and wearing a pale, emotionless sack over his head. With long, spindly fingers and gangly legs, the Boogg slinks through the night, seeking children to steal. Other stories tell of the Boogg luring children out of their beds and into the surrounding forests, enticing them with warm homes and plenty of treats to eat. This aspect of the Boogg's story would eventually help to inspire the Grimm Brothers's fairy tale "Hansel and Gretel" as well as the twenty-first century's Slenderman.

> The Boog was the closest I came to my truest form. Often, I would forget how terrifying I could be in this foggy shape with my white eyes. Sometimes, all it takes is a passing glance in the mirror to remind oneself of our true potential. And sometimes, all it takes is a passing glance in the mirror to remind oneself that we're monsters.
>
> —From the diary of Tenebris, The Boogeyman

THE NØKKEN

IMAGINE WALKING A beautiful pathway through thick woods when you hear the distant strains of a lovely violin playing in the distance. You hear it plainly and find that you need to find its source. It is not an option, you *must* find the source of the beautiful music echoing throughout the forest and along the river's edge you follow. As the music grows louder, you see the man sitting on a stump near the river, violin wedged gently under his chin as his bow lightly caresses the strings. His handsome face is wrought with intensity as he feels the music he plays for you, and before long, you are standing less than a foot from him, swooning to the seductive delivery. Your eyes droop closed, and you're lost in his dulcet tones. But then the music stops, and you feel a hand on yours. Soft at first, but quickly tightening. The warm skin turns cold and clammy, and when you open your eyes, you find yourself staring into glowing yellow eyes. The white, soft skin of the man has turned bluish, cold, and wrinkled. His smile has become a frown filled with razor-sharp teeth. His soft brown hair has become black, matted, and stringy.

And you're still in its clutch-es as it drags you helplessly into the water. You are at the mercy of The Nøkken, and only one thing can keep him from stopping you forever . . .

A dangerous and manipula-tive creature from Norwegian folklore, *Nøkken* is a name derived from the old Norse word for "seahorse" yet there is very little that is benign or fantastic about The Nøkken. He is a horrid creature who feasts on the flesh and souls of those unfortunate enough to be drawn in by him. Everything about The Nøkken is manipulative, from his shape-shifting appearance to the enticing water lilies abounding near his lair. His favorite prey are women and children, who often stop by the water to pick or admire the floating flowers.

Once he's seduced you with his look and his beautiful music,

Ernst Josephson's 1884 painting depicting the Nachen in human form with his violin. To the Swedes, this portrait embodies the pure essence of the Nachen. (*Painting by Ernst Josephson. On permanent display at the National museum in Sweden.*)

he uses his true appearance to render you paralyzed with fear as he drags you beneath the water, never to be heard or seen again. But if you were to call him by his true name, he would most certainly release you and return to his home in the waters once more.

But that doesn't mean The Nokken isn't benevolent at times. Legend has it that if you were to shed three drops of blood, offer up a flagon of vodka, or sprinkle snuff into the water, The Nøkken would accept the offerings and teach you how to play his music as elegantly as he does. Its not nearly as terrifying, but it's something to remember if you're ever in Norway and want to get music lessons on the cheap. This facet of The Nøkken closely resembles that of another folktale in Norway, that of the Fossegrimen, the water spirit of a violinist who sold his soul in exchange for formidable talents as a player.

In his brilliant and incredibly detailed book, *The Esoteric Codex: Shape-shifters*, Gary Melhorn brought to light one of the more famous and magical stories about the Nøkken. The old tale dealt with a Norwegian fisherman who lived near the Fagertärn Lake with his wife and his beautiful young daughter. While the fisherman tried hard to provide for his family, the lake yielded very few fish. As he sat in his canoe on the lake and prayed for fish, he was approached by The Nøkken who promised to deliver huge multitudes of fish in exchange for his daughter the day she turned eighteen years old. The fisherman agreed, and The Nøkken delivered on his promise. When the fisherman's daughter turned eighteen, she went to the lake shore to meet The Nøkken, but when she saw him, she took a knife and swore that he would never have her while she still lived. Stabbing herself in the heart, the daughter fell into the water, dead. Her blood mingled with the water and turned the white lilies red, a color they have stayed to this very day.

An interesting derivation of the legend of The Nøkken is that his appearance sometimes foretold tragic drowning accidents. In certain spots of a lake or river, The Nøkken would screech, and a fatal drowning would later take place in that exact spot. But over the years, the horrid legend of The Nøkken would soften a bit with the onset of Christianity; instead of stealing people down to his watery lair, The Nøkken would sob and sing songs of woe about how he would never be a child of God, a perversion of the original folktale that was changed to reflect a more Christian outlook.

"Although Christianity forbids such offerings, and pronounces the old water-sprites diabolic beings," writes Jacob Grimm of The Nøkken in his 1888 book, *Grimm's Teutonic Mythology*, "the common people retain a certain awe and reverence, and have not quite given up all faith in their power and influence: accursed beings they are, but they may some day become partakers of salvation."

Jacob Grimm always liked to hear himself talk. One could never shut him up, unlike his brother Wilhelm, who barely spoke a word. Probably used to not getting a word in while his brother was around. I admired his passion for the monsters of the world, however. And it was a passion for the fantastic, not a blood lust. He was an advocate, never an enemy.

— From the diary of Tenebris, The Boogeyman

THE MARE

OUR DREAMS ARE where our greatest desires come to life. We're what we've always wanted to be in the realm of dreams, but what about the terror that comes from a nightmare? Is it everything we fear come to light in a boundless, un-waking realm of pure imagination, or is it the work of something more diabolical, one that squats at our bedside and poisons our dreams into crushing nightmares? Perhaps, if one were to believe in the horrifying wraith known as The Mare. Evil and unrepentant, The Mare is seen as an evil spirit or goblin who straddles the chests of sleeping men, women, and children, bringing on horrifying nightmares. Though her legend spans numerous regions, countries, and belief systems, The Mare was first written about in the thirteenth century by Norse storytellers, described as a ghostly, hideous spirit that preyed upon the insecurities of kings and noblemen, essentially riding their chests as they slept. The nightmares brought on by this nocturnal nymphet often resulted in the kings misinterpreting the dreams as omens of good fortune, when they were in fact, the exact opposite.

Jacob Grimm, one half of the famous Grimm Brothers, studied the legend of this spirit extensively in his 1883 book *Teutonic Mythology*, likening The Mare and other crafty ghosts to gods, goddesses, and demi-gods not unlike those from classical Greek mythology. He also compared The Mare to the more popular, much more benign Norse ghost, the Vættr.

The Mare would enter the room through the keyhole in the door, her ethereal spirit wafting through the night air before returning to her original form. Sitting upon the chests of her sleeping victims, The Mare would strangle, torture, and molest them until their dreams became nightmares. The victim would wake bruised, frightened, and bloody with not a single clue how they got that way.

In later years, children were advised to make the sign of the cross on their pillow, or sleep facing a window in order to repel a Mare. Still others contend that one only needs to put an upsidedown broom next to the door or sleep with their belts lying across the sheets. In German folklore, The Mare could be kept away by saying a simple prayer:

Here I lie down to sleep
No night-mare shall disturb me —
They must swim through all the waters
That flow upon the earth.
And then must count all the stars
That appear in the sky.
(Help me God, Father, and Holy Ghost)
Amen.

The Mare's influence today is, of course, found in the word "nightmare," which encapsulates just about every fiendish, ghoulish, and horrific dream anyone has ever had. But according to the early Norwegians, all of these bad dreams have only one mother: The Mare, who still rides the night to this very day, bringing horror to the land of dreams.

THE HORROR OF TROLLS AND ELVES

IT ISN'T TOO much of a jump to go from night demons and creatures to the puckish lives of elves and the brutish worlds of trolls, and while the elf mythos is incredibly detailed and multifaceted, The Boogeyman's contribution to elven horror came in the form of Dark Elves, impish creatures who used nature as camouflage and the life-force of humans as their favorite beverage.

Such legends of Dark Elves span a multitude of cultures, but as long as we're still in the general region, lets focus on the more horrific ones centered around the rural dark lands of Germany, Iceland, and Britain. The elves of J. R. R. Tolkien's Middle Earth are a bit of an anomaly in the entire mythos; his flaxen haired, gentle, god-like warriors were almost too pure to be real, while in other folk tales, elves were darker, dastardly, devious, and extremely cunning, daring to seek out human souls to slake their otherworldly thirsts.

Stories of elves originated in Germany, but spread across Europe, taking root in England and portions of The Netherlands. Medieval tales told of beings with magical powers and supernatural beauty. Their blase attitude toward humans made them even more mysterious, and it was thought that they would use their power to help or hinder humans in need. Germanic and Old English stories consider them to be separate creatures capable of monstrous harm, whereas Old Norse tales ranked them on high, almost on a level playing field with the gods.

One of the most compelling and chilling tales of an elf's strange, horrific power comes in the form of "The Erl-King Poem," written by Johann Wolfgang von Goethe in 1782 as part of an opera called *Die Fischerin*. In the story, a frantic father races on his horse through the night, his son lying in his arms. While the son seems to see and hear things that aren't there, the father assuages his sons fears by agreeing with him, even though he doesn't truly believe it. When the son exclaims that he's been attacked, the father rides faster to his home, only to discover that his son has died in his arms, the victim of an attack by the Erlkonig (or "Elder King"). It is generally assumed that Goethe was referring to elves in "The Erlking Poem," especially when one looks at his inspiration for it. "The Erl-King's

Daughter," written as a ballad in 1695, laid the fault at the feet of the Erl-King's child rather than the Erl-King himself. By contrast, female elves were thought to be vindictive, jealous, and hungry for revenge against human men. Seducing wayward men traveling on the dark roads, elven women often lay with these men, who in turn fathered monstrous children, and ultimately left them cold. In this way, it could become the reason why the father's son is attacked in Goethe's poem. Perhaps he had a tryst with a female elf and left her, provoking an incredible rage and streak of jealousy within her.

The arrival of trolls and elves marks the first time The Boogeyman began to parse out his responsibilities, and it was a wise choice on his part. The world was growing, undeveloped lands were becoming civilized, and it was hard to be in so many places at the same time. From this need to tap fear from the humans, Tenebris created trolls, gnomes, and goblins, though it was a tenuous relationship at first. Many of his representatives turned on him, choosing to defect to the other side; they became ambassadors of goodwill and peace.

But the others, those remaining few, found solace in terror and became agents of fear. Like the Greek gods before them, these new creatures sprang forth from Tenebris in the dark lands of Scandinavia, from the memory of Grendel. From there, they migrated in different directions, finding homes in Britain, Germany, and Italy. Others, like the trolls, remained in their homelands, staking claims under bridges and inside desolate caves. Their work is the stuff of legends, and they no doubt made Tenebris proud.

Trolls are one of the most written about creatures in Scandinavian folklore, often described as old and strong, but slow-witted or dim. In the beginning, people reported the appearance of trolls as being fairly human-like but with thoroughly antisocial behavior. As years progressed, however, the description of a troll became a bit more fantastic. Early Christians tended to demonize them, referring to them as hideous, Godless creatures. But this was not by choice, only by design. They are creatures of nature, not unlike the pagans who worshiped the Sun and Earth, effectively making them Godless creatures in the eyes of Christians. They revered nature, living among the animals, flora and fauna, and fairies. But to cross a troll meant taking your life into your own hands. An offender of the earth would be dealt with harshly.

The darker trolls, on the other hand, cared about their surroundings but held an extreme hatred of human beings, those hairless, handsome creatures that always thought they were better than everyone else. They found shelter in dark, wet places and often used the fear humans had of them to their advantage. They would place themselves into situations where contact with humans was inevitable, such as the classic bridge troll tales, for no other reason than to mess with them. Trolls were also incredibly vindictive if they were wronged, dispensing horrific punishment to those who would slight them to even the smallest degree. But being slow-witted, the trolls could also be tricked into falling for their own greatest weakness. As evidenced in books and fables like *The Hobbit* and *Grimm's Fairy Tales*, trolls are susceptible to sunlight, rendering them into stone. The Troll Wall in the Romsdalen Valley is one living example of this legend, for it is said that two armies of warring trolls got so caught up in their warfare that they both forgot the time and

Trollveggen (the Troll Wall), the highest vertical cliff in Europe at more than 3,600 feet, is seated in the Romsdalen Valley in Norway. Legend has it that the wall was created when two warring armies of trolls were caught in the sunlight in the midst of battle, turning them into the huge wall of stone that sits there now. (*Courtesy of the Library of Congress Photochrom Prints collection.*)

were caught outside when day broke. The massive armies turned to stone, creating the 3,600-foot wall that now sits in the middle of the valley, a formidable cliff popular with BASE jumpers and folklorists alike.

In the face of fearsome creatures such as trolls, however, common sense and quick wit sometimes eludes humans. One such story is that of Finkee, a Danish troll living among farmers in the southeastern Jutland area of Denmark. Supposedly, a set of mountain ranges and hills lined the area and everyone knew that trolls lived in these cavernous mountains; nightly parties made the caves and mountains light up with firelight and the sounds of merriment. One day, a farmhand was passing by and decided to tease the trolls by throwing a rock into one of the nearby caves. A troll angrily ran out, bellowing, "Tell Finkee that little Kee is dead!"

The farmhand had no idea what the troll was talking about, but when he returned to the farm that night and told all of his friends what had happened, the story fell on ears they didn't even know were there. The troll named Finkee had been living on the farm secretly for many years, but he never forgot his troll kin living in the mountains and hills. Apparently, the stone thrown into the cave had struck one of the little troll children, Kee, killing him. Angered by the senseless murder of the child, Finkee cut the throat of the farmhand and left the farm forever.

But one thing that has not changed about the troll is the sheer size of them. In some stories, trolls are mountainous beings that often pretend to actually *be* mountains, surprising defenseless travelers, fishermen, and playing children. This race of trolls is actually more playful or mischievous than the darker, more brutal trolls who hide in the dark, watching and waiting for someone—anyone—to pass his or her path. These dark trolls have no conscience and an undying hunger for flesh and bone. They would soon become more brazen, stalking the streets at night, peering into windows. Just as the human contempt for nature grew, so did the troll's contempt for humans. Stories passed around fires and bedsides told of trolls who ate little children because the meat was more succulent. Rumors persisted of trolls who could smell the blood of Christians before it had even been shed, allowing them to hunt them down more easily and devour them before bloodcurdling screams could perforate the night's silence.

THE PESTA

IN SEPTEMBER OF the year 1349, during a dark and dismal night, a ship drifted into Bergen Harbor on the shores of Norway. It was accompanied by eerie and baleful silence; only the creaking of its timbers and the muted squeal of rats in the hold could be heard. As it drifted into port, workers nearby boarded the mysterious ship from England, only to find the entire crew dead, their ulcer-riddled bodies strewn recklessly all over the ship. In the scant amounts of time it took for the ship to sail with its cargo of wool from England until it sailed dangerously into a Norwegian port, the hideous Bubonic "Black" Plague or Death had infected the crew and killed them all painfully and quickly. Only the rats in the hold, the ones carrying the disease, survived. And when the hold was opened, the rats fled and disappeared into the Norwegian cities, villages, and woods, spreading the dreaded plague quickly. Infected fleas riding piggyback on the rats soon jumped from their hosts onto humans, who spread it farther and farther into more civilized locations. In time, it was said that the plague decimated roughly two-thirds of the population of Norway before being halted.

With the arrival of the Black Death, so too came the Pesta, a haggard witch-like creature who others thought was only a propaganda-like symbol for the pestilence plaguing European countries during the fourteenth century. Starting in 1346, the Black Death reached the shores of Scandinavia only a few short years after breaking out in Central Asia. With it came the mysterious appearance of a deathly pale woman with glowing white eyes, body swathed in black, and hands seen carrying a rake or broom.

Given the name The Pesta, after the Latin word "pestilence" meaning "plague," she stalked the lands of Denmark and Norway with a devilish passion to unleash hell and suffering upon the land. Traveling from farm to farm, she would dole out her judgment without impunity or remorse. If she was seen carrying her rake across the farmlands, only a few of the farm's residents would die. But if she were seen carrying her broom, it was a sure sign that all who resided there would fall to the Plague. In any case, if she was seen, death would be following behind her.

Through valleys of life and death, I have seen the destruction of humans, though I cannot control who lives and who dies, for I am only a consequence of such calamity. I am there when all else has failed and died, when all hope is lost, when the wellsprings have dried out, when all that remains is fear and loathing. I task the human spirit to find strength in its remaining resources, no matter how dark, and move along. I am a necessary evil.

—From the diary of Tenebris, The Boogeyman

THE BYSEN

IN THE WORLD, there are mascots and symbols for just about every group imaginable. So, too, this holds for the boogeyman as well, for the creature known as the Bysen is said to haunt the woods of Gotland Island near Sweden. He is sort of an anti-patron saint of woodsmen, causing problems for humans just trying to do their jobs in the Swedish woods. Gnome-like and peculiar, the Bysen is said to be a cursed human, condemned to walk the earth forever as a gnome, ax slung over his shoulder, guarding over the woods he is assigned to watch. His crime? Cheating other men out of their land by moving the marking stakes that separate one patch of land from the other.

And "mischievous" doesn't even begin to describe this tiny terror.

Reminiscent of a hippie gremlin, the Bysen will snag your attention and make you follow him, only to get you hopelessly lost in the woods. He does this for no other purpose other than for his own entertainment. Woodsmen in ancient times blamed the Bysen for their carriage wheels breaking, or for their massive loads of lumber toppling over unannounced. Using the visage of a stump as camouflage, the Bysen works his way in and around the world of humans deftly, spreading mischief and mayhem as well as Tyler Durden ever could.

Folklorists say that the Bysen has been seen walking across properties in the woods, moving fence lines back into place, muttering to himself, "This is right, this is wrong," as if he is trying to undo the wrongs he committed in his previous life as a land-grabbing human. In addition, if a human were to follow behind the Bysen, correcting the wrongly placed sticks, the Bysen would finally gain peace and his curse would end. It's a fairly elaborate, yet startlingly inane, twist in a very odd tale indeed.

Incidentally, the Bysen is known on the Swedish mainland as well, though there he is called something far worse and far more terrifying: *Osaliga Lantmätare*, which is Swedish for "unholy land-surveyor."

> I claim little responsibility for the Bysen. He was the product of Loki's twisted imagination, a "boogey-trickster" if you will, for mischievous natures are only the beginning of what I do. However, it was I who sent him properly on his way into the woods. I can appreciate a good folly when I see one, and nothing is funnier than when a human—who thinks of himself as almost as mighty as the deity he worships—becomes hopelessly lost in the woods. It is hysterical. It never grows tiring.
>
> —From the Diary of Tenebris, The Boogeyman

THE DRAUGR

FROM THE PLAYFUL stunts of the Bysen, we end our tour of Scandinavia with one of the most horrifying tales in Old Norse folklore, and one of The Boogeyman's greatest disguises. It was a creature that would inspire not only the zombie and vampire genres, but also the fearsome Nazgul in J. R. R. Tolkien's *Lord of The Rings* and the White Walkers in George R. R. Martin's *Game of Thrones* saga. Called the Draugr, they are literally the walking dead whose will to continue on is stronger than the bonds of death. Seeking refuge and shelter in their hastily dug graves, they are thought to be guardians of treasures that had been buried with them, but their true destiny is far more personal.

Draugr are mostly known for having died tragically or unexpectedly, either through murder or suicide, and their need to rise from their graves nightly to seek vengeance upon the living is brought on by their anger and need to complete unfinished business. They covet life and seek to torment those who have it. The Draugr are not dissimilar from ghosts in this way; they can shift from physical forms into wispy spectral forms easily, but retain their physical bodies in their natural state. Their skin tones range from pale, icy blue to dark shades of magenta with eyes glowing intensely white.

One aspect of the Draugr that particularly unhinged a lot of people was the fact that, following their death and resurrection, the Draugr's body would enlarge to astronomical proportions, swelling to two, maybe three times their original size, resembling trolls or small giants with misshapen heads, arms, and legs. For this reason, The Draugr did not need to carry a weapon. His entire body was his weapon, using it to crush his opponents before devouring them whole.

"The undead corpse was rendered yet more terrifying by its propensity to swell to enormous size," says Christie Ward, aka the Viking Answer Lady. "This property of the undead was apparently not due to gasses released by decay, for the body of the draugr was also found to be enormously heavy, and was often described as being uncorrupted, even many years after death."

But being assaulted by it wasn't the only means by which The Draugr tormented people; just being around them was enough to drive normal people completely insane so that they might destroy themselves. Draugrs, like the legendary Thorolf, delighted in killing birds just by having them fly over his grave. People driven to insanity by the Draugr would often kill fellow villagers indiscriminately before finally committing suicide. Of course, their suicide would often result in them becoming Draugr themselves, thus preserving the line of marauding Draugrs for years to come.

As if it couldn't get any worse, the Draugr became adept at shape-shifting, a talent once reserved exclusively for highly talented witches and warlocks. Using the human's empathy for animals, The Draugr would turn themselves into lame cattle or benign kittens, masks used to hide their insidious nature, for once they had been taken in by a benevolent human, The Draugr could very easily dispatch them and maintain complete anonymity. Other times, they would use the superstitious villagers' worst nightmares to their advantage, transforming into repulsive trolls that would easily tear their prey limb from limb.

So how can one tell which grave houses a Draugr, and which grave does not? According to Norse folklore, the grave mound of a Draugr would glow as if a fire burned beneath it. But slaying a Draugr was much easier said than done, for the Draugr were impervious to weaponry of any kind, and only the most courageous and formidable hero could even stand to face him. The only way to vanquish a Draugr was to wrestle him back into his grave, rendering him powerless. The hero would then behead the Draugr, burn its body, and dump the ashes into the sea.

In order to keep the recently deceased from becoming a Draugr, a pair of open iron scissors were placed on the chest of the dead. Their big toes were tied together so that they might find difficulty in walking. Finally, their grave was bricked up so that if they *did* rise from the dead, they would not be able to exit the grave as easily as if it were simply a dirt mound.

> How I loved the Draugr. Their methods were harsh and bloody, but effectively terrifying. After I birthed them, I chose not to align myself with them, but there was obviously a professional admiration between us. My favorite parts are when the grave robbers chose to meddle with one of the Draugr's graves. I can still hear their screams when the Draugr woke, and the thieves realized their mistake.
>
> —From the diary of Tenebris, The Boogeyman

CHAPTER TWO

THROUGH THE DARKENED MISTS OF AVALON

THE UNITED KINGDOM

I traveled to the British Isles in stories told by frightened men; they carried me with them inside their souls. A tiny part of me remained with them for eternity, gestating in them until their bodies gave out. But not before passing me off to their children. And their children's children. Life among the Britons was as ripe with superstition as it was among the Norsemen, but in this case, the souls of Britons hadn't hardened as much as the Norsemen's had; it was far easier for my legend to procreate and take flight.

—From the diary of Tenebris, The Boogeyman

JUST AS THE Black Plague had spread from country to country, so too did the tales of Tenebris. By now, he was known by many different names, but they were all roles played by the same creature, plotted and executed by the same beast. He stopped first in Scotland, then Ireland, and finally in Great Britain, and at each stop, Tenebris had an imposing effect on the indigenous peoples. Scots and Irish alike heard Scandinavian tales of horror at port side villages, trading posts, and pubs, and it wasn't long before these creatures were given lives of their own, stalking the green countryside swathed in mist and shrouded in night.

The highlight of this evolution was that now, the creature soon to be named The Boogeyman would no longer be content in hiding in the shadows of caves, forests, and bridges. He would now be lying among them as they slept, slithering in and out of darkness, listening to their ever increasing heartbeats, sniffing their growing fear as it poured from their skin. The British Isles afforded Tenebris the opportunity to spread his wings and create a diverse group of creatures for each region that was as different as the last. From witches and warlocks, to devil dogs, rat-faced men, banshees, and dragons, each island in the United Kingdom had a different devil to face each night when they lay their heads down to sleep.

THE BLACK ANNIS

BLACK AGNES, OR simply Black Annis, may not be one of the oldest legends in English folklore, but it certainly is one of the more disturbing ones and one that actively recalls the legends brought to the Isles by Norse traders. Reeking of the influence of Hans Christian Andersen and The Grimm Brothers' tales of ugly, evil witches, Black Annis's tale dates back to the 1700s and a mysterious parcel of land known only as "Black Anny's Bower." This land sits near the Dane Hills, bordering the Leicester Forest, and the "bower" in question refers to a large cave near the mouth of the forest. Some believe the cave leads to a faerie world where human children are taken after faeries steal them from their beds. Other folklorists believe it to be a sacred Druid cave system used for centuries to perform blood sacrifices to Danu, the Celtic Earth goddess and wife of Ludd, the sky god.

The legend of the Black Annis is an amalgam of both of those legends and far more terrifying than one could possibly imagine. In this branch of the legend, Black Annis is a child-eater, a blue-faced crone with iron-tipped fingernails and a nasty temperament who roams the Leicester countryside at night. She is said to be the harbinger of winter, haunting the snowy night, seeking out wayward children and sheep who had traveled too far from their homes. Her intent was to not only devour their flesh but harvest their skins as well. After drinking their blood, the Black Annis would skin them and hang the bloody tissue from the oak trees outside her cave. After they became brown and stiff from the sun and wind, she wore the skins like a macabre apron around her gaunt waist.

Needless to say, the very idea of what the Black Annis would do to them kept children of the area very securely in their beds at night. While many people point to mythological demi-gods, such as Greece's Demeter (goddess of the harvest and mother to Persephone) and India's Kali (Goddess of Time, Change, Power, Creation, Preservation, and Destruction) as the true origin of Black Annis, her actual legend seems very firmly rooted in reality.

Author Ronald Hutton declared in his book *The Triumph of the Moon: A History of Modern Pagan Witchcraft* that the Black Annis was actually a medieval nun by the name of Agnes Scott. She'd dedicated herself to Christianity and the Roman Catholic Church, spending much of her adult life tending to the sick in a local leper colony. With the advent of the Protestant Reformation, her legend was twisted and turned into a sick tale of witchery and murder. Over the years, the name Black Agnes would be softened and twisted as well, eventually becoming simply Black Annis. Agnes Scott's connection to Black Annis was deepened when it was revealed where she had been born and raised: in the cave outside Leicester Forest in the Dane Hills, the area commonly associated with the baneful Black Annis.

Sightings and tales of the Black Annis continue to this day, holding a superstitious grip upon the folks of Leicester. Children of the Second World War told stories of how she would chase them as they collected wood near her cave while they hid out with their families trying to avoid the massive German bombing raids that were decimating the larger cities at the time.

More recently, the legend and look of the Black Annis no doubt inspired George R. R. Martin when he created the terrifying White Walkers for his *Game of Thrones* series of books, complete with blue faces, translucent eyes, and a knack for appearing at the onset of winter.

> Caves and caverns, forests and thickets . . . naturally dark all the time and given new menace by my children, and what could be greater than that? The promise of bloodshed in the event of trespass. No quarter earned, no quarter given. Ever.
> —From the diary of Tenebris, The Boogeyman

THE CŴN ANNWN AND THE BLACK SHUCK

IF WITCHES AND crones preying on the fears of Britons lie securely at the top spot of the boogeyman's food chain, then the idea of an enormous demon-like dog takes a very close second, for no other beast has inspired more horror than the tales of the Cŵn Annwn and the Black Shuck, two very similar legends with very different stories. The mere idea of demon-like animals is even more terrifying to some for their inability to be reasoned with, for they serve no other master but their hunger and cannot be swayed by tears or laments for mercy because they simply cannot understand the language of humans.

Based solidly in the countrysides of Wales, the Cŵn Annwn (pronounced "Kune Anoon") is often seen as two large, brutish mastiffs with flame-red eyes and rancid breath. For many, the true origin of the Cŵn Annwn comes from the Welsh folktales of Annwn, a mysterious fairy world ruled by Arawn, king of the Welsh underworld. The Cŵn Annwn ("Hounds of Annwn") were Arawn's faithful hunting companions in the Welsh countryside, centered mostly around the mythic mountain of Cadair Idris near Dolgellau, Wales. Their baneful howling and ferocious barks were loudest when at a distance, and softest when they were at their closest to the prey. In essence, the Cŵn Annwn are not evil dogs, nor are they truly "hounds of hell." To the people of Wales, Arawn was king of a faerie world, an underworld of magic that teemed with fantastic life, one that promoted peace and justice. In this case, the Cŵn Annwn's goal was merely to hunt down criminals and chase them until they could run no longer, just as the criminals did to their victims.

Again, sadly, with the arrival of Christianity, the Welsh legend of the Cŵn Annwn was perverted in order to convert as many pagans as possible, and the moral cleansing of the criminal element was erased from the story. The Cŵn Annwn was relegated to the dark folktales of Banshees and Witches, evil creatures that fed upon the Christian faithful. The Cŵn Annwn were now seen as portents of death, devilish Hounds of Hell that served the dark lord Arawn, who now had become the mythical king of the dead.

The Black Shuck, by comparison, was Tenebris at his most dastardly and horrifying. There was no denying the intent of the Black Shuck's legend, for he was born from the Briton's terror of feral dogs. Covered in fog and mystery, the moors and highlands of the United Kingdom became ripe with tales of Orphic, baneful creatures intent on feasting upon the fear and morality of humans. Many have described the Black Shuck as having only one fiery red eye, while others have described him as being "headless," but by far, the most popular accounts tell of an enormous, pitch-black hound with two fiery eyes. Heavily muscled and equally fast, the Black Shuck was known to have frequented dark roads and empty footpaths. He was said to be as big as a horse or full-grown bull and the thick black hair on his back would rise up when he snarled and growled. His howl is ominous and filled with expectation, quite unlike the searching yowl of the common timber wolf. He walks without a sound through the night, so quietly that some believe he walks upon the mist itself. The legend of the Black Shuck quickly became a popular story, instilling fear in the foolhardy and giving the cautious reason to be even more so. Like most stories of that ilk, the tales were told to make children behave and convince criminals and highwaymen to change their devious ways and stay off the roads.

The most infamous story of the Black Shuck took place at two churches on August 4, 1577, in Bungay and Blythburgh near Suffolk. The Black Shuck burst through the doors of the Holy Trinity Church in Blythburgh to the accompaniment of a loud thunder clap. Running up the main aisle, the ghost dog was said to have killed one man and a young boy before causing the steeple to collapse. The Black Shuck escaped the church unscathed, leaving behind fiery paw prints that marked his trail of flight. That same day, Reverend Abraham Fleming of the neighboring St. Mary's Church in Bungay attested to seeing the Black Shuck running all about the interior of his church, killing two as they were engaged in silent prayer. In a downright spooky development, archaeological excavations performed at the ruins of St. Mary's Church, in 2014, yielded the remains of what appeared to be an enormous dog. Archaeologists estimated the dog weighed at least 200 pounds and stood over seven feet tall. But was this the Black Shuck of legend, or was this the dog that inspired the legend itself? As of this writing, carbon dating is still being done to determine the actual age of the bones, though other artifacts uncovered in the same area can be traced to the year 1577, the same year the Black Shuck went on a complete rampage.

Ghostly and terrifying, the Black Shuck also foretold the deaths of those who were unlucky enough to see him in all his glory. But just as many people who claimed to have seen the Black Shuck and lost family to death within the year, the same number went on to continue their lives uneventfully. But when it came to women, the Black Shuck seemed to have developed a rather protective role. Tales have been told of the Black Shuck accompanying women to their homes as they walked alone at night, essentially seeing them safely to their doors and disappearing into the darkness once they set foot inside. This seems to have been the way the Black Shuck would end up in legend, for eyewitness accounts of the

Shuck have him approaching humans benevolently, especially as the nineteenth century turned into the twentieth century.

> Dogs of the modern world are so docile and lovable that I fear many will be unable to divine the reasons why phantom hounds were so terrifying once. But I tell you this: the greatest fear produced by dogs come from the human expectation that such a creature will turn on them, that the wildness will remain and take over once more. That is what gave birth to the Cŵn Annwn and the Shuck. The greatest antidote for that? Treat them well and love them forever. Dogs are not born bad; they are made that way by those who fear and exploit them. One would not blame a human for retaliating against abuse. Why blame an animal? Perhaps this is why the Shuck and the Cŵn Annwn are revered more than feared these days.
>
> —From the diary of Tenebris, The Boogeyman

THE DULLAHAN

> That Irving fellow completely stole my legend from me, using it to rather great effect in his short story, "The Legend of Sleepy Hollow." Though I would have preferred to have been credited, it can be safely assumed that readers no doubt thought of me when they turned their lights out and went to bed after reading it. And I was there, I was always there. And I'm still there.
>
> —From the diary of Tenebris, The Boogeyman

TENEBRIS'S INCARNATION AS the legendary headless rider in Irish folklore no doubt did encourage Washington Irving's story of "The Headless Horseman of Sleepy Hollow," but Irving needed the option of exposition and back story to frighten his readers. Tenebris, as The Boogeyman, did not. There was no need for anyone to know why fear existed and why the dark was so terrifying. Truly, the dark was terrifying because of what people put there: their own ghosts and demons populated the caliginous phantom zone like vengeful wraiths seeking out new hosts. Ireland, for instance, has a broad, storied history, one filled with whimsy and matched only by tales and legends of war and bloodshed. Continuing battles and conflicts against the English battered the serene countryside and made ghosts of millions of Irish men, women, and children. In that despair, like so many other battle-scarred countries, there grew legends and tales of fallen warriors and villains, mythic frights created to help deal with real horrors.

The infamous Headless Horseman, depicted in John Quidor's 1858 painting, was directly influenced by tales of the Irish phantasm, the Dullahan. (*Painting by John Quidor. Original on display at the Smithsonian American Art Museum.*)

Such a legend is the one that grew out of the Irish realm of faeries, appearing from the ashes of war in the mid-to-late 1600s. Called the Dullahan (which itself means "dark man" in old Gaelic), this headless ghost of war drives a carriage pulled by two black steeds through the Irish countrysides, his head nestled perfectly under his arm. Though the body drives the cart, the head is clearly the one in charge. The Dullahan's eyes are tiny and black, darting about the night as they ride in search of the one they mean to announce as next to die. The skin of the head is loose and creamy and maintains an amber translucence, and its jagged smile seems to reach from ear-to-ear. The rider, meanwhile, is said to have been seen brandishing a human spine as a whip, and the carriage in which they drive is fashioned from human bones. But unlike Irving's Horseman, the Dullahan is legion; there are many who perform the same task all over the Emerald Isle, and just because one is seen on the coast terrifying villagers doesn't mean that one won't appear outside your own window.

Tenebris hit a home run with the Dullahan, imbuing him with supernatural powers and a fiery temper worse than a redhead on their birthday. Doors and locks that were closed to him would mysteriously open, and those who watched him on his rounds would find themselves soaked in blood tossed from a basin by the Dullahan himself. Other stories claim that he would whip their eyes, blinding them as he drove past. To say he didn't like to be watched while he worked was an understatement that was not lost on Irish citizens.

But when the Dullahan stops his carriage, the once silent severed head opens its gaping maw to issue forth a name in an unmistakable bellow that rattles the roots of trees and sends chills throughout the land, for the person he names immediately perishes before the Dullahan can even drive the carriage away.

Though the legend spans the country, Dullahan sightings had mostly been relegated to the counties of Sligo and Down, remote parts of Ireland still rich in folklore and seasonal traditions. One of the more famous accounts of the Dullahan comes from Irish storyteller W. J. Fitzpatrick, who encountered the Dullahan at sunset when he was a small boy: "I seen the Dullahan myself, stopping on the brow of the hill between Bryansford and Moneyscalp late one evening, just as the sun was setting. It was completely headless, but it held up its own head in its hand and I heard it call out a name. I put my hand across my ears in case the name was my own, so I couldn't hear what it said. When I looked again, it was gone. But shortly afterwards, there was a bad car accident on that very hill and a young man was killed. It had been his name that the Dullahan was calling."

Like all great monsters, though, the Dullahan do have their weaknesses. In this case, the element of pure gold is said to cause the Dullahan to abscond without claiming a victim; travelers are warned to carry even a small bit of gold with them if they walk the dark roads at night, especially at times of Irish feasts or festivals. Stories of the Dullahan sprouted from the legend of Crom Dubh, an ancient Celtic god who demanded bloody human sacrifices in exchange for incredible fertility of womb and farm. The preferred method of sacrifice? Beheading.

The worship of Crom Dubh (aka "Black Crom") would continue all the way until the sixth century when, again, Christian missionaries arrived on the island and immediately put the kibosh on all things pagan and witchy.

For this treasonous act, Crom Dubh was not pleased. He sent forth his emissary, the Dullahan, to collect the blood and souls Crom Dubh had been denied when the Christian influence became too much for the pagans to ignore. He was the embodiment of death, the right hand of a bloodthirsty god. Unstoppable and irrational.

It was a brilliant tale and Tenebris knew it. Soon, the Dullahan was appearing everywhere, the pitch black silhouette of his carriage appearing in the moonlight, pointing his all-seeing severed head into the windows of terrified Irish folk, praying to God they did not hear their name called out by the envoy sent by the god they had forsaken.

THE RATMAN OF SOUTHEND

WE COME NOW to a legend of the boogeyman that rose from the ashes of a tragic death, a wrinkle in the folklore that would inspire horror films and novels for generations, for the Ratman wasn't born of a god, nor was he the product of a faerie world. He was British refuse that declined to be swept under the rug. Like most countries in the world, there is an underworld of poverty that leaks into the middle class on occasion and that underworld breeds as many monsters as an imaginative campfire.

Centered around the town of Southend-on-Sea in Essex, the Ratman's lair is said to be a tunnel-like underpass that connects various pedestrian walkways along the roadside. These tunnels were popular with the homeless of Britain who used them regularly as shelter from snow, rain, and wind. The tunnels became dangerous ground for pedestrians passing through for that reason, becoming the sites of muggings, rapes, and the occasional murder at the hands of these destitute men and women who had nothing to lose and everything to gain.

Located on Sutton Road near the Mayor's house in Sussex, the underpass tunnel now nicknamed "Ratman's Tunnel" is said to be different than the other tunnels of the area. A homeless man, well known to the area and those who lived there, commonly sought shelter there. During the day, he would be milling about the area panhandling and trying valiantly to score a kebab from local food vendors, but at night he would curl up against the tiled wall of the tunnel and sleep through the night in relative peace. But one night, a group of teenage boys came through the tunnel, drunk and looking for a fight. They found it in the old man, who they beat mercilessly and almost to the point of death. They left him alone finally when they found he couldn't stand on his own anymore. After losing an incredible amount of blood and unable to stave off the cold, the old man died. Passersby found him the next day, still curled into a ball, lying in a sticky pool of thick blood, with a nest of rats chewing away at his stiffening flesh.

It wasn't long afterward that locals began telling stories of hearing strange noises coming from the tunnel, such as high-pitched squealing and the eerie sound of long fingernails scratching against the smooth tiled walls. People began to use other tunnels instead of this one; most felt uneasy in the tunnel and others claimed to have seen odd-shaped shadows following after them. Most of the stories seemed too fantastic to be true and the Ratman became a scary story to tell in the dark.

However, no one truly knows that when they feel as if they're being followed in that tunnel, they really are being trailed by something else.

Tenebris was there that night when the homeless man he knew only as David was attacked, and it was Tenebris who went to his aid in the dark. This was an act Tenebris had never perpetrated before and it would be the last time he would intervene in the matters of the human world.

> When I had seen the brutality of those humans and how they wailed upon the poor man, I felt rampant disgust and anger in myself for the first time. I went to the old man—David— as he lay dying and I put my hand to his cheek.
>
> "What do you want?" I asked him.
>
> He looked at me and said, "I want to die. But I want to stay too." He wanted to stay after he died, becoming an Earthbound spirit. This was a covenant between him and God and I had no business infringing on that pact. God gave him what he wanted, but I left him with the power to proliferate a horrifying legend that would keep people from coming upon his land forever. The power to terrify at will using all that had been done to him as tools against trespassers. He'd earned that power and I was not going to deny him.
>
> —From the diary of Tenebris, The Boogeyman

SCOTLAND'S BEAN-NIGHE AND THE BANSHEES OF IRELAND

AS WE COME to a close on the adventures of Tenebris in the United Kingdom, we are reminded of a legend that Tenebris himself admits to being born of "a ridiculous night in Mull and Tiree, where all I did was try to come up with the most ridiculous incarnation of fear that I possibly could. Granted, I'd come up with some doozies in Norway and a few in the Germanic mountains, but nothing compared to the Bean-Nighe."

Like the Dullahan, the Bean-Nighe (pronounced "ben-nee'-yeh") heralded death in one of the most stupefying ways possible. Let it first be said that the Bean-Nighe was a very gifted creature in many ways, the most prominent one being that she was incredibly well endowed. So well endowed was she that the enormity of her breasts impeded her work as a washer woman of death shrouds, so to combat this, she took to tossing her breasts over her shoulders as she worked, preparing the shroud of doom for the person who would be called to wear it before the night was over. Her preferred location was at the seashore, using the rough currents of the ocean and the rocks on the beach to facilitate her cleaning of the death shroud. Legend has it that if a man was able to sneak up behind the Bean-Nighe and put one of her nipples into his mouth, she must tell him the name of the person who was to die that night. Doing so would postpone the death for whoever the shroud was intended for, if only for a short time.

But sneaking up on the Bean-Nighe wasn't an easy task, and those who failed to accomplish this would face horrible misfortune at her hands. Scottish folktales tell of boys, girls, men, and women approaching an old woman from behind on the beach, only to have the old woman turn and throw the shroud upon them, effectively marking them for death before the night was through. The Bean-Nighe was often described as being rather short and squat with a withered, mean face. Her bare feet were webbed like a duck, and they clung fast to the rocks of the beach so the incoming tides would not take her to sea.

> She was similar to The Ratman, in that Bean-Nighe was the spirit of a woman who had died far too soon, usually in child-birth. She would remain the Bean-Nighe until her spirit reached the age at which she was supposed to have died in life. The first Bean-Nighe was a beautiful young girl named Beira, but in death she became withered and crone-like. I always found it sad that she had to mourn the deaths of others before she could mourn her own, but most people forget about that. They only tend to remember the "nipple thing" when they reminisce about the Bean-Nighe.
>
> —From the diary of Tenebris, The Boogeyman

Traditionally, during the funeral of an Irish citizen, a woman would sing a song of mourning called a lament. It was almost always a signature staple of the Irish funereal process and these women, known as "keeners," could fetch a hefty sum for performing only one song. For the upper-crust families of Gaelic royalty, the "keeners" at their funerals would be actual faeries, sent to pay homage to fallen members of illustrious families. Because these faerie keeners had the gift of foresight, they would often sing their songs of lament before death had even reached the intended victim.

But unlike the Bean-Nighe, the non-human Banshee couldn't be reasoned or bartered with; her appearance outside the homes of wealthy Irish families was a fact of life in which they braced themselves. The original Irish Banshee was thought to be named Aibell and stood as the ruler of twenty-five other Banshees who would be sent off to different regions depending upon the needs of Aibell. Sometimes, families would hear the wail of numerous banshees across the Irish countryside, calling on multitudes of Irish souls. This was especially true during battles and wars when numerous Irish nobles would face death defending their lands from invading English armies.

Early nineteenth-century newspaper illustration depicting the Banshee. (*Artist unknown.*)

However, like most tales of terror, there is another tale, one grounded in reality, that explains the origin of the Banshee and links her more closely with that of the Bean-Nighe. It is said that she is the ghost of a young woman who was brutally murdered and, having died so horribly, was condemned to wander the earth, warning others of their own doom.

Their appearance resembled the classic "lady in white" specters of later folklore, having long flowing white gowns and equally pale hair. Described as being "hag-like" or withered, she has also been described as uncommonly beautiful and radiant, almost too beautiful to look upon. In both cases, her mouth is always seen opened in a state of permanent screaming, wide and horrifying, with eyes filled with sorrowful terror.

> My influence in creating the Banshee was limited to her spirit form and her unnerving tactics, but I was happy to let her spread her wings and do her business. Lovely girl, but one could never hold a decent conversation with her in any cause.
>
> —From the diary of Tenebris, The Boogeyman

CHAPTER THREE

THE TRUE HEART OF DREAD

THE EUROPEAN ABYSS

Eastern Europe . . . shadows crept out of that region the likes of which I had never known. Finally, a place that matched the darkness of my own center. Fear had been a part of them for so long that they were hardened to much of what the world already saw as true evil. That was exhilarating: finding the true heart of their dread and exploiting it.

— From the diary of Tenebris, The Boogeyman

A S THE SHADOW of Tenebris crept slowly over the European continent, he finally felt as if he'd found a match for darkness in the mountains and woodlands of Eastern Europe, specifically the countries of Germany, Russia, and all those in between. Already plagued by folklore of vampires, witches, and child snatchers, the Eastern Europeans proved to be a mighty challenge for our Boogeyman. How do you terrify a region already so traumatized by darkness?

It was a task Tenebris embraced, naturally. After not finding much success with different incarnations of vampires, shape-shifting beasts, and the occasional troll (an act he borrowed from his time in Scandinavia), Tenebris tested the waters of an as-yet untouched fear: the loss of a child. For this experiment, he tested the waters in Hamelin, Germany.

THE PIPED-PIPER OF HAMELIN
HAMELIN, GERMANY
1284 AD

It was early morning when I first set eyes on the little town and even though I was still miles away, I could hear the shuffle of the rats in the streets and under the rough-hewn houses and cottages. Several months prior, the Black Plague, a sickness brought on by fleas clinging to the hides of the rats, had begun its century-long internship of Europe, decimating entire villages in a matter of weeks. Here now was Hamelin, a village not unlike the others on the verge of becoming a mass grave.

I'd chosen my disguise early on, that of a wiry flutist, clad in mostly in red robes with a large floppy hat that covered much of my face in shadow and the tail feather of an owl jutted out from the brim of it. Now pale and gaunt, I clutched my instrument in hand and walked down the hills into Hamelin. The sounds of the rats grew louder and louder, and soon I heard not only the shuffle of their paws, but also the rancid squeak of their voices mewling among each other. I approached the Mayor's house (which I had deduced simply because it was much larger than the others) and rang the house bell mounted outside the front door.

The door opened to reveal a corpulent, nearly blind man dressed in a fine sleeping robe with an elongated smoking pipe in his hand.

"Are you the mayor of this propinquity?" I asked as the Piper, bending a knee in salutation.

"I am," replied the Mayor, his voice rough and not at all jolly.

"Your honor, sire, I am a man of many talents, though my greatest is the fastidious removal of rats."

The Mayor cocked an eyebrow. "Are you, now? Plenty of those around here. Each time we eradicate one nest, two more seem to pop up. And their numbers increase three-fold each time! Tell me, how do you remove them? Fire? Drowning? It's Toadstool powder, isn't it?"

I shook my head and smiled. "I play them music, my lord," I told him.

The Mayor snorted. "Sir, I believe you're pulling a prank on me."

"Oh no," I said. "No, indeed I am not. I will remove every rat you have here for the low, low price of only two bags of silver. Sir, my process is guaranteed."

The Mayor reluctantly agreed to the terms, more so because he was curious to see me fail. But like I said, my process was guaranteed, and I turned from the Mayor and walked to the center of Hamelin. By now, a great crowd had swollen the streets and people were leaving their little homes to see this curious man in red who somehow commanded their attention. Putting the flute to my lips, I began to play, soft at first, and then louder once I noticed the rats begin to congregate in the streets.

My playing turned playful and jaunty as hundreds of thousands of rats emerged from their holes and surrounded me in the center of town. They were falling over themselves, climbing up my stockings, trying to get as close as possible to the source of the music. The villagers were both horrified and awestruck at the sight of all of them, these vermin who now trampled each other just to get closer this "Pied-Piper."

Slowly, I turned and began to walk through the streets, my slip-pered feet careful not to tread upon any of the excited rats milling about the path. Slowly and deliberately, playing softly and hypnot-ically, I led the rats of Hamelin out of the village and into the near-by Waser River, where each and everyone of them drowned. All but one. This one, I thought as I picked it up by the tail, will live on to tell others what happened here. And with that, I released the one rat and watched it scamper away from Hamelin, thankful for its life.

Turning round, I walked back into the village and bowed before the Mayor.

"I have fulfilled my part of the contract. Now, please be the honorable man I know you to be and fulfill yours."

The Mayor snorted again. I gathered that this had to be his version of a laugh, yet I found it difficult to understand what was so funny. His fate had been sealed the moment I was sent here.

Villagers balked at the idea of giving up their hard earned mon-ey, and they voiced it loudly. "Pay him nothing! You had no bargain with us, Piper!"

The Mayor, as well, seemed keen on retaining as much of his money as possible and he said, "You drowned all the rats, you did, indeed. Quite a sight it was, too." The Mayor took a step toward me. "But now that they're all gone, drowned in the Waser, what is my impetus to pay you? Are you going to resurrect them all and plague them upon Hamelin once more? I think not. Take your pipe and leave this place."

I knew it was coming. Indeed, this was why I had been sent to Hamelin. I hadn't wanted to make an example of them, but now I

Medieval painting of the Pied Piper of Hamelin. (*Artist unknown.*)

felt as if I had no choice; as I walked away from the Mayor, I noticed the multitude of children clinging to their parents. As my eyes set upon them, I cryptically warned, "You will see me again."

I walked out of Hamelin and disappeared over the hills. For months afterward, the villagers of Hamelin went about their daily lives, forgot about me and my warning. They got comfortable with their betrayal. They had seen this slender, almost fragile man in red and immediately assumed that he couldn't retaliate. But had they seen my true face, they may have thought differently. I had truly hoped that the people of Hamelin would do the right thing. I had hope for them, but like all of my missions into the world, I was prepared to do what I had to do. In the end, the people of Hamelin forced my hand; their unrepentant sins were nails in their casket lids.

I returned to Hamelin during the Christian holiday of Saint John and Peter's Day, which fell on June 26. The holiday, used to commemorate the end of the Apostles' fasting period, called for mandatory attendance at the local churches. The church service began in the early evening, culminating with an all-night vigil at midnight followed by a Divine Liturgy in the morning. Children weren't allowed at these services and they were left at home with nannies or older siblings in charge.

This was why I chose this day to return.

Now dressed in hunter green, I entered Hamelin for the last time, playing my Pipe in the still night. As I walked slowly through town, as I passed each home, one by one, the doors opened and the children of Hamelin stepped out in the streets following after me in a daze. By the time I'd made my way out of Hamelin, 130 children were following behind me, swaying and dancing ethereally to the music of the flute. Where I took them will remain a mystery, but they never returned to Hamelin. Ever.

— From the diary of Tenebris, The Boogeyman

The legend of the Pied-Piper grew, quickly becoming a hard-learned lesson in keeping one's word, an oft-old morality tale used to encourage others to "pay the Piper." Graven images of the Piper didn't show up until about 1384, when a church in Hamelin commemorated the 100th anniversary of the event by placing a stained glass window depicting the Piper into one of their windows. It remained there until the destruction of the church in 1660. In all honesty, the true meaning of the commemorative glass window is up for debate. An inscription in the glass read, "In memory of the 100 years since our children left us." The truth behind the cryptic saying is completely unknown and points to numerous concepts.

Theorists over the years have scoured history for rational explanations of the event, suggesting that the children died due to plague, while others have said that the children were lured away from their homes by pagans and taken into the forest to ritualistically dance before falling into a massive sinkhole. Poems, songs, and stories ran rampant across Germany and most of Eastern Europe. One document that stands out was known as "The Lüneburg Manuscript," penned by a monk named Heinrich of Herferd between 1440 and 1450 AD in Lüneburg, Germany. It is widely considered to be the oldest recorded story of the Pied Piper, placing the disappearance of the children at the "koppen," a Germanic word for "knoll" or "hill," one of several surrounding the village of Hamelin. He also specifically mentioned the Piper by name for the first time, giving the flutist his famous moniker.

Poet Robert Browning, in an 1842 poem, speculated that the Piper led them into a mystical portal, lost forever in a great unknown, and the tale of the Piper became one of the most popular stories spread about by the Brothers Grimm. Stripping away the mysticism and fairy tale bits, one can almost see that the story of the Pied Piper is a metaphor for the Black Plague, which decimated significant portions of the European population. Brought about by infected fleas piggybacking on the millions of rats breeding across Europe, the bite from the fleas infected humans with a dangerous, often fatal pox that resulted in boils, bleeding, fever, and eventually, the complete shutdown of the body's major organs.

An even more rational explanation comes from the city of Hamelin itself, who have proclaimed on their website that the children were part of a massive exodus of immigrants who left the area in order to settle parts of Eastern Europe. Historical documents in Romania support this influx of people from the lower areas of Germany. In addition, legendary linguist Jürgen Udolph claims to have found the descendants of the Hamelin children living in Poland. Cross referencing names from the original census taken in Hamelin, Udolph found nearly every single last name of the Hamelin children living in present-day Poland, supporting the theory of a mass emigration.

Even to this day, the burg of Hamelin prohibits music and dancing on the Bungelosenstrasse, the street where the children were purported to have been last seen before their iconic disappearance. And every June 26, the Hamelinites celebrate Rat Catcher's Day instead of the more secular Saint John and Paul's Day. Rat Catcher's Day also seems to have inspired the United States to declare July 22 National Exterminators Day.

Today, the idea of a Boogeyman being a child stealer or cradle snatcher is fairly common, and it all began with The Pied-Piper.

> I consider the job in Hamelin to be my most inspired role. It was the
> first time—but not the last—that I played a human. I think I pulled

it off pretty well. And no, I'm not telling you what really happened. There needs to be *some* magic left in the world. You wouldn't believe me anyway.

—Tenebris, The Boogeyman

(Interview #1, 10/31/2015)

The relative cleanliness of The Pied Piper led Tenebris to then call upon the more grisly portions of his imaginations. He was, after all, capable of darker, much more grave terrors than that of a stocking-clad flutist in a floppy hat; it was a trait he prided himself on, and while the Pied-Piper was a resounding success, Tenebris soon ached to return to his more macabre, blood-caked roots.

The presence of the vampire in folklore and literature is perhaps almost as old as time itself, for many believe that Lilith, the first wife of Adam from the Book of Genesis, essentially became the world's first vampire temptress when she disobeyed her husband and was cursed by God for her insolence. Folktales circulating throughout the Middle East would tell tales of her blood lust and sexual prowess. So the vampire legend was hardly Tenebris's idea; moreover, it was a grim reality of the dark world. They *did* exist. And they were repulsive creatures, created by Satan himself and ushered forth into the world quietly and without much fanfare. Their lust for blood and theatrics caused Tenebris to take notice, and he thought, "That's good. But I can top it."

THE NACHZEHRER
AND THE STRIGOI

GRAVEYARDS CAN BE terrifying places. There are spots in the United States where cemeteries or graveyards are absolutely beautiful and stammeringly tranquil. But there are also graveyards that are more than a bit overgrown, untended, and forgotten, which lends a true creepiness to a once-placid resting place for thousands of bodies. The universal fear of death and what happens after permeates these places, and it was here that the boogeyman cultivated what was possibly his most disgusting creating, the vile Nachzehrer (pronounced "Not-zerror").

In the cemeteries of Germany, caretakers began to find graves dug up and the corpses inside looked to be half-eaten and defiled by some grotesque creature. Calling the offending creatures Nachzehrer, which literally means "after night" in old German, the moniker only alluded to what time of day the creature appeared. The true purpose of the Nachzehrer was much, much worse.

While vampires were human-like and drank the blood of the living, the Nachzehrer were found to be partially decomposed, monstrous vampires who sought out the meat of the dead, gorging themselves on decomposing flesh. Most certainly a vampire but with traits closer to a ghoul or a modern-day zombie, the Nachzehrer could be found plundering graveyards across most portions of Northern Germany and also in parts of Poland and Bavaria. While most legends and myths of the world exist simply because they exist, the Nachzehrer, like the Vampire, has an entire back story and medical history. According to German folklorists, the Nachzehrer are created after death, usually from those who committed suicide or died accidentally. Their affliction is not blood borne or viral, but is seemingly pre-ordained; their sins dictated their fate in the afterlife. Some legends swear that babies born with a caul will become Nachzehrer upon their deaths.

Upon awaking from their death sleep, the newly born Nachzehrer will attack and devour its death shroud as well as its own flesh. As it eats and as its hunger increases, the living family members of the Nachzehrer will begin to take ill and die as well, becoming a fresh food source for the Nachzehrer. Caretakers and visitors to the graveyards would find open graves with partially or fully consumed bodies and bones lying inside. Some blamed animal scavengers, others blamed the Nachzehrer. One thing was certain, however: if there was a grave found that contained a body holding its thumb in its opposite hand with its left eye open, it was most certainly a Nachzehrer and needed to be dealt with immediately before it could rise again in the night, plunder more graves, and cause more family members to fall ill.

Killing the Nachzehrer for the final time entailed placing a coin in its mouth and cutting off its head. When I asked Tenebris about the coin, his answer was concise, though similarly baffling:

> The coin made of gold rendered the Nachzehrer into a state of palsy, allowing the executor to dismantle the body starting at the neck. I was—and still am—profoundly befuddled that the humans were able to figure that one out. But for every ten Jonathan Harkers, there is a Van Helsing standing behind him, one who will always figure it out despite how cryptic I make the cure.
>
> —Tenebris, The Boogeyman, (Interview #3, 10/31/2015)

At the height of Nachzehrer fever, German folk began to bury their dead with stones filling their mouths, spikes driven through their heads, or without their heads entirely, all in an attempt to prevent them from rising from the grave and causing their surviving families more distress and illness. Eventually, these methods became entwined with classic vampire lore and the notion of the Nachzehrer was lost almost entirely, replaced by classy, charismatic creatures of the night with a flair for Victorian fashion and heavy eyeliner.

> But they *never* sparkled. Vampires and Nachzehrer do *not* sparkle, I promise you.
> —Tenebris, The Boogeyman, (Interview #3, 10/31/2015)

And speaking of the vampire, we move now to Romania, the unquestioned home of the vampire legend to look on Tenebris's next invention, the Strigoi. But in this case, the Strigoi not only survived legend, they became real for millions of Romanians who still believe in them to this day.

The Strigoi ("stree-goy"), which is a Romanian variation on the word "scream" and it seems to suit the nature of the Strigoi perfectly, who are described as being the troubled souls of the dead who have risen from their graves to cause a multitude of problems for the living. But moreover, the Strigoi can also be human, transformed by other Strigoi, and can possess all the powers of a classic vampire, but is still able to manipulate the spirit world. Imagine it: a vampire with all of its powers *and* the powers of an evil spirit.

It's okay to shiver at the thought. Scream, if you have to. I'll wait.

The Strigoi legend goes back all the way to Pagan times and the lore of Dacian myths. The Dacians ruled a section of Romania and Transylvania near the Danube River and surrounded by the Carpathian Mountains. In that time, the Strigoi were evil spirits denied entry into the good kingdom of Zalmoxis. Left alone on Earth to their own devices, they soon found plaguing mankind with all kinds of trouble to be the best way to pass the time. The types of mischief the Strigoi would get up to would be the equivalent of a poltergeist-type haunting today. As oral tradition watered down the finest details, the Strigoi became simple blood drinkers who would stalk the living. They would be seen more as close relatives to vampires than the spirits they once were.

Romanians, Croatians, and Slavs alike have recorded horrifying encounters with creatures they believed to be Strigoi, including Jure Grando, a Croatian who was beheaded, in 1672, after he terrorized his village following his first death in 1656. Similarly, Serbian peasant Petar Blagojevich returned as a murderous Strigoi, butchering his own son who refused to feed him upon his return. Even as late as 2003, Romanian funeral parties included drunken trips to the graveyard to properly dispose of suspected Strigoi, only in this case the "hunting party" was arrested and charged with "disturbing the peace of the dead." They paid damages to the offended family and as a result, morticians drove fire-hardened metal stakes through the hearts of the dead before burial, in an effort to be sure they were really dead.

The Strigoi would soon find immortality in films like *Nosferatu*, *'Salem's Lot*, and *What We Do in the Shadows*, portrayed as thin, gray, and rat-like, a far cry from the ethereal charm of Count Dracula, but closer to what a true vampire might look like, as one might hope. Let's face it: A vampire such as the Strigoi is a thousand times scarier than a smooth-talking European aristocrat with a penchant for stealing wives from oblivious husbands.

THE LOUP GAROU

FRANCE HAS ALWAYS been known as the refined and classy capitol of Europe, but they themselves are not without their charms either. Aside from giving us the best fried potatoes ever and the most incredible variation on a simple kiss, the French have their own monsters in which they contend with as well. Tenebris, while admittedly not a fan of French culture, still chose to make his mark on this country in some way, though that "way" wasn't entirely clear; once he'd crossed the border into France, he found his thought processes had completely bottomed out, essentially becoming a diabolical case of writer's block.

> Artists and creators don't flock to Paris and to France in general, they are born there. Which is possibly one reason why I found myself listless and bored. Artists take fear and use it to create. I never wanted them to create miraculous representations of what I happened upon them, and I could not reckon any kind of mayhem that would *not* be turned into some form of fancy-dancy art for their museums and palaces. It was as if they were taking their screams and turning them into "oohs" and "ahh's." *That* was disturbing."
> —Tenebris, The Boogeyman, (Interview #3, 10/31/2015)

For more on Tenebris's influence on their "fancy-dancy art," see the Appendix at the conclusion of this book.

Listless and bored Tenebris remained until he had conjured a mysterious beast that he set upon the Margaride Mountains of Gévaudan in the south-central portion of the country. Attacks from the so-called "Beast of Gévaudan" would continue for three years, and his cryptic methods led innocent villagers to believe that this beast was either a twisted human being or simply a hungry wolf. Still, either option was terrifying, and the stories he heard in the dark coming from little children and their parents gave him hope that nightmares could soon be coming as long as he played his cards right.

The Beast of Gévaudan, for those not in the know, was the name given to the animal or creature that plagued the Margaride Mountains in Gévaudan, France between 1764 and 1767. The attacks became so frequent that the French government stepped in, supplying the region with armed troops

1512 woodcut illustration of a "werewolf." (*Artist unknown.*)

and commandeering the security forces of local Nobles. Victims were discovered with their throats torn out, ripped to shreds by powerful jaws that looked to belong to a large dog or wolf.

Over the years, the exact number of victims claimed by the Beast of Gévaudan has fluctuated, but most experts on the subject agree that out of 210 attacks, 113 of them fatalities. The remaining 97 victims survived, but few of them could accurately describe the beast itself, counting the darkness and the surprise of the attack as factors. What details *did* emerge painted a fearsome portrait of a devilish creature: a wolf as big as a calf with a large, dog-like head and ears that swooped straight back. It had a robust, barrel chest and its fur was dark red except for a thick swath of black running down its hunched back. When it opened its mouth, two huge rows of razor-sharp teeth were exposed, held together by a massively muscular jaw.

The Beast of Gévaudan was eventually killed on June 19, 1767, by a local nobleman by the name of Marquis d'Apcher, who used a handcrafted silver bullet to bring down the creature everyone was convinced was supernatural. All doubts that this was the wolf responsible for the attacks were laid to rest when human remains were found inside the dead animals stomach.

This was hardly the first time a werewolf legend had been tossed around; in 1591, in medieval Germany, Tenebris himself had afflicted a local villager named Peter Stubbe with a lycanthropic malady that made him change into a wolf-like creature each night. But here was a chance to improve upon that fairly simple design. By creating the Loup Garou,

Tenebris effectively changed how people viewed werewolves and abridged the once carved-in-stone legend forever.

Much of the same aspects of the werewolf remained in the Loup Garou (which is literal French for "werewolf"), but instead of relying on the cycle of the moon to change form, the Loup Garou could become a wolf anytime he or she pleased. Not only that, but they retained their human thought processes and intelligence. Vengeful Loup Garou could target enemies, rivals for a lady's hand, or silence a witness to the madness, all the while knowing that a wolf would be blamed for it and not the human. In an already paranoid world where people couldn't be trusted anyway, here was a creature that could not only hide among the humans but also hide their secret well and for indefinite periods of time. There could be a Loup Garou living next door. He could have been your father, your mother, or your best friend.

Only death would reveal the secret of the Loup Garou, for wolves killed by humans returned to their human forms as they died. But killing a Loup Garou doesn't end the carnage and terror. The curse of the Loup Garou is passed on to the one who killed it. For 101 days, they must live in secret silence of their condition, for if they speak of the Loup Garou, they will walk the Earth forever as one of them. But if they are quiet about the affliction, and wait out the 101-day quarantine of silence, they remain human and are free to carry on with their lives.

All of these complex rules gnawed at me a little and I once asked Tenebris why he felt the need to constantly make his creatures full of stipulations. His answer was simple: "It is more fun that way, watching them stumble over a rule, then hurriedly go back to pick it up, seeing them get flustered. And then there is the off-chance that one will break one of the rules and you get to see a real show, one that hundreds of kiddies will unwittingly see and remember forever. Fairly delicious stuff and it makes for a good time. At least for me."

The legend of the Loup Garou would eventually travel across the world and into America, becoming a hugely popular Cajun myth in Louisiana. In these cases, the Loup Garou would hunt down Catholics disobeying the rules of Lent. So before you have a hot dog on Friday during Lent, remember: the Loup Garou is watching. And waiting. Waiting. And watching . . .

THE GOLEM

I'd portrayed religious entities before. The snake in Eden was my first assignment when Satan was still in charge of all things Boogey-

ish. He lost those rights in 900 BC to the Greek Fates in a lucky game of pinochle, which at the time was called The Game of Earthly Rounds and it was played with papyrus leaves dyed different colors instead of the more modern playing cards. Anyway, after successfully tempting those two bone-bags in paradise, I was given the role of this misshapen Jewish avenger, which worked out well early on (especially during that rather infamous incident in Prague,) but their belief in me waned and I was relegated back to the shadows. Oh, the misery I could have avenged during your World War II.
　　　　　　　　　— From the diary of Tenebris, The Boogeyman

THE FAITHFULLY RELIGIOUS are quick to squash anything demonic under their heels, but all religions have their own avenger of sorts. The Muslims have Ifrits and Azazel, mystical Djinns who follow the faith of Allah and afflict unbelievers. The Christians really don't have a moral avenger outside of Jesus Christ, but the religious belief in Saint Nicholas would eventually spawn tales of The Krampus (which we will get into later).

The Jewish faith, however, is rife with avengers, including The Nephilim (half human/half angel beings who watch over the Earth,) Lilith, (the demonic first wife of Adam who was cursed by God for not obeying her husband) and Samael, the Jewish archangel of Death. But perhaps the most well-known avenger in Talmudic Jewish folklore is the story of the fearsome, nearly unstoppable Golem. It could be said that tales of the Golem were inspired, at least in part, by the bronze giant Talos in Greek mythology. Standing several stories high, the bronze statue was created by King Minos of Crete as a guardian of his kingdom. Until he was destroyed by Jason and Medea, his main goal in life was to toss boulders onto ships attempting to invade the island. Even in that guise, the animated metal-guardian took his job of protecting the kingdom very seriously.

The Golem of Jewish lore walks the same path as Talos, seeking to protect and aid his people. Formed into the shape of an enormous man, the clay Golem is brought to life through Jewish mysticism, using secret rituals that very closely emulated the birth of Adam in the Book of Genesis, that being the formation of a man using dust or mud and brought to life by the power of God himself. Early stories of the Golem illustrated him as being bulky, enormous, and simple-minded; he could not speak and responded only to the Rabbi who created him. Usually, the Golem was created to right a specific wrong done either to the Rabbi himself or to his people. A closely guarded and secret folktale, the tales of the Golem didn't become available to common men and women until the Middle

Ages when the Jewish Book of Creation was studied by alchemists and mystics across Europe in hopes that they too could create a Golem. But the complicated Jewish texts and the general disregard for the proper rituals and punctuation of Jewish words made each attempt a failure. It wasn't until around 1630 when Rabbi Eliyahu created what was arguably the first recorded Golem in the annals of legend. A Polish Jew and practitioner of Kabbala, Rabbi Eliyahu allegedly created a Golem from thick clay found on a nearby riverbank. Named Emet, the Golem was brought to life and sent back to dust when his name plate was removed from around his neck.

> As an aside, I'll mention here what I heard from my father's holy mouth regarding the Golem created by his ancestor, the Gaon R. Eliyahu Ba'al Shem of blessed memory. When the Gaon saw that the Golem was growing larger and larger, he feared that the Golem would destroy the universe. He then removed the Holy Name that was embedded on his forehead, thus causing him to disintegrate and return to dust. Nonetheless, while he was engaged in extracting the Holy Name from him, the Golem injured him, scarring him on the face . . . the legend was known to several persons, thus allowing us to speculate that the legend had indeed circulated for some time before it was committed to writing and, consequently, we may assume that its origins are to be traced to the generation immediately following the death of R. Eliyahu, if not earlier.
> —Rabbi Jacob Emden, 1748
> from *Megilat Sefer: The Autobiography of Rabbi Jacob Emden*

While Jewish folklore is chock full of references to the Golem, it was what Tenebris describes as "that incident in Prague" that solidified the Golem as a classic monster for the ages, inspiring nightmares in Jews and Gentiles alike. Most people try to portray reigning emperor Rudolf II as the instigator of the Jewish desperation, but the reason for that is only because Rudolf II had a genuine interest in the occult, alchemy, and the arts. In truth, the Jewish despair began in 1580 when a notoriously shrewd and deceitful Christian priest by the name of Taddeush developed a plan to vilify the Jews by accusing them of ritualistic murder, a charge that would lead to their execution and expulsion from their homes. Rabbi Loeb, a very well-respected and revered Holy Man, discovered the plot and prayed to God for an answer to the threat from Taddeush. God, in response, sent him a message from Heaven.

"Ata Bra Golem Devuk Hakhomer VeTigzar Zedim Chevel Torfe Yisroel," which means "Make a Golem of clay and you will destroy the entire

Jew-baiting company." Sounds easy enough, but hidden in the words were directions only a learned and faithful rabbi could decipher, which Rabbi Loeb did using techniques from Kabbalistic formulas. After days and days of rituals and purification, Rabbi Loeb and his sons went down to the River Moldau and formed the Golem out of river clay, its gaze looking to Heaven. A piece of parchment, known as The Shem, was inserted into The Golem's mouth, upon which was written the name of God; placing or removing the parchment would either activate or deactivate the Golem. After reciting prayers and Hebrew incan-

Early eighteenth century illustration of the Golem and its maker. (*Illustration by Mikolas Ales, 1899.*)

tations, the Golem lit up bright red, then went gray again, with water flowing from his body. It grew fingernails and hair before standing to its feet before his new master, Rabbi Loeb, who named him Yossele, the Hebrew pronunciation of "Joseph."

But one rule that had to be adhered to was the strict regulation that the Golem be deactivated on Friday evening so that he would not be guilty of desecrating the Sabbath on Saturday. One Friday night, Rabbi Loeb forgot to remove the Shem, allowing the Golem to roam free while all other Jews were in their homes preparing for the Sabbath. The Golem went on a murderous rampage, killing numerous Gentiles in the Prague ghettos and surrounding areas. Rabbi Loeb, being the only one who could actually control the Golem, cornered his creation outside of a synagogue and pulled The Shem from his mouth. The Golem immediately fell to the ground and broke into several pieces. Knowing that he could not risk allowing the Golem to return, Rabbi Loeb stowed the body of the Golem in the attic of the synagogue, where it lay for centuries. No one was allowed to enter the attic in any way. Those who have seen the inside of the attic, however, have said that they saw no Golem, yet were convinced that they had seen the chalky clay outline on the floor where it had once lain.

So if the Golem wasn't in the attic, where is he?

> The Golem was reclaimed by the Hebrew God, who saw the foolishness of man and knew he couldn't be trusted with such power anymore. But it never stopped me from using that likeness later on, even just a few weeks after the initial "incident." So while I was

never responsible for the deaths in Prague, I did enjoy using the likeness to terrify Jewish children into observing the Sabbath properly. Good times, good times.

—From the diary of Tenebris, The Boogeyman

Tenebris, in the guise of the Golem, would go on to terrorize children in Lithuania as well as other portions of Czechoslovakia. The Golem legend would even inspire "The Gingerbread Man" stories of the Slavic regions, becoming a baked pastry that came to life after a lonely old woman baked him while pining for a child. But perhaps the most famous reinterpretation of the Golem legend came when Tenebris visited a young woman in her dreams while she vacationed in Geneva, Switzerland with her poet husband in May of 1816. The dreams she had, where a pale, hideous phantasm continually chased after her would inspire her to write one of the most terrifying novels of all time: *Frankenstein*.

BABA YAGA

WITHOUT HER, THERE would be no Blair Witch, The Sanderson Sisters, or perhaps even a Bell Witch of Tennessee. There would be no real threat inside the story of "Hansel and Gretel," nor would there be any uneasy terror left in the tale of H. R. Pufnstuff's "Witchiepoo." Those stories would still be there, of course, but undoubtedly influenced by some other horror. What separates the Baba Yaga from Welsh, Norse, and Celtic witches is her unrelenting assault upon the nervous systems of those involved.

Created by Tenebris in the mid-1450s, the legend of Baba Yaga grew slowly until it became a fixture in Russian and Slavic countries around 1755, creating a wave of terror the world had not known since the emergence of the Gorgons of Greece and the Banshee of Ireland. Modeled after the Black Annis and Bean-Nighe, Tenebris went out of his way to make the Baba Yaga as memorable as possible. At first glance, her world seems to be made from all the imaginings of folklorists who imbibe in smoking too much pipe-weed in the middle of the day.

Tenebris, however, denies any such imbibing and almost took offense when it was mentioned.

Baba Yaga is described almost universally as tall, gangly, with six-foot-long arms and equally large, bony legs. Her nose is pronounced and capable of smelling humans entering her forest within seconds of the beginning of their journey. Stringy hair and pallid skin that hangs loosely from her bones complete the picture of the Baba Yaga, allowing us to see a fairly hideous creature capable of great harm to trespassing humans. Looking on her legend today, she is the quintessential witch, always looking to trick a succulent human into her oven or cooking pot. In some tales, however, there are three Baba Yagas, all sisters, each of them as spiteful as the last. They work in tandem to tire their prey before attempting to snare them in

Russian artist Viktor M. Vasnetsov's acclaimed portrait of the Baba Yaga carrying off a victim. (*Painting by Viktor M. Vasnetsov, 1917.*)

their vile clutches. But to the one who touches her heart the most, the Baba Yaga can be as maternal and loving as the best mom in the world, nurturing and caring for her prey as if he or she were her own child.

Her home, nestled in the deepest parts of the forest, is as much a sight to behold as the Baba Yaga herself. It stands on magical chicken legs and is capped with the head of a rooster on the roof while a fence made of human leg bones surrounds it. Those brave enough to venture into her hut are taken aback by the size of her oven, which stretches from one end of the hut to the other. It is an oven large enough to cook a grown man whole, for if the captured human fails to finish any of the tasks assigned to him by the Baba Yaga, he will be filleted and cooked on the spot.

The tales of how she managed to capture, imprison, and trick humans into becoming dinner usually revolved around the hero of the story, but Baba Yaga's influence was never lost. She became a real threat to children who tended to wander off alone, and parents found that invoking her name kept their wayward children close.

"Baba Yaga has witchy traits, and the witch in nursery lore often stands in for the female ogre, sharing some of her characteristics, though she is seldom built on the ogress' Brobdingnagian scale," writes Marina Warner in her book, *No Go The Boogeyman*. "Instead she can take the shape of a bird or a cat or a simple old woman, like the jealous queen in Snow White."

DER SCHWARZE MANN

There is merit to those ideas [of racism and its beginnings], but it is hard to excuse someone's rampant hatred of another race by blaming it on a harmless Boogeyman from prior generations. The stigma of the word "black" is only bad if you allow your perception of it to be bad. Racism is a personal holocaust that can be ended quickly if only people would fear *me* instead of their neighbors.

— From the diary of Tenebris, The Boogeyman

FEAR DOESN'T DISCRIMINATE. It affects everyone differently, or not at all. Fear is primal, fear is universal, innate. Like most of the monsters Tenebris has become, fear is the overwhelming result. However, while fear is subjective, only one of Tenebris's guises can be linked to a massive cultural degradation. Sometimes fear can be taught, sown into the souls of the young, and evolve into something a thousand times removed from its original intent.

Such is the case of Der Schwarze Mann ("The Black Man"). The legend of The Black Man, or Der Schwarze Mann, began around the Middle Ages, and not once did his ominous moniker ever refer to the color of his skin. Rather, Der Schwarze Mann's name came from the dark places in which he liked to hide. In this way, he reminds us of the classic "monster under the bed" or even Rawhead and Bloody Bones, a gruesome monster we'll discuss later.

Der Schwarze Mann was most often classified as one of the fabled "Kinderschreck Monsters" or "child-frighteners" in German folklore and legend whose sole purpose was to just simply scare the bejeezus out of children. His tale is fairly bland compared to those of Baba Yaga and Rawhead, but being a mostly generic boogeyman gave Der Schwarze Mann the opportunity to become anything that the child was afraid of, whether it be as a cloaked stranger under the stairs or a mist-like wraith swirling around their ankles as they walked to the lavatory.

But Der Schwarze Mann's favorite hiding spot was in the deep, dark woods that Germany is most famous for, hiding among the trees and brush, looking to stalk and terrorize children foolish enough to walk alone at night. But Der Schwarze Mann was fairly benign; he wasn't known to be a child-snatcher or child-eater. His motive was just to scare, so it seems logical that he would become the subject of a children's game known as *Wer Hat Angst Vorm Schwarze Mann*? Or, "Who's Afraid of The Black Man?"

Locals of the area and some historians believe that he was a strange resident of the Black Man mountain in the Eifel region of Germany. But his most likely origin came during the Black Plague of Europe in the Middle Ages. The man responsible for removing the dead plague victims would enter the homes dressed completely in black wearing special headgear resembling a mask with a large, protruding beak. The appearance of the man, who was called Der Schwarze Mann, triggered anxious fear in nearly everyone, for if the Black Man was in town, so was the plague.

While Tenebris's creation was never meant to instill a racist belief, it is unfortunate that a lot of people believe that it seemed to contribute to a growing fear (or in the very least, a severe distrust) of African and Moor immigrants to the region in later years. Proponents of racial equality still believe that the fear of the black-clad Der Schwarze Mann seemed to lead directly to the misguided fear of physically black men and women.

> I grew tired of witches, vampires, and shape-shifting devils in the dark, so what came next felt completely liberating and intoxicating, for when I stepped into the Asian society, I was free to reinvent myself for a whole new culture of fear. It was delectable and the memory of it is delicious still. They were frightened of the same things, but not in the same way. It sounds as if there is very little difference, but there is. There really, really is."
>
> —Tenebris, The Boogeyman, (Interview #4, 11/01/2015)

CHAPTER FOUR

FEAR ETERNAL

TENEBRIS INVADES ASIA
AND THE PHILIPPINES

The people of Japan, China, Korea, and even the Philippines could
be counted on to be as superstitious as the Europeans, but taking
them to the brink of madness with their fear, to the point of suicide,
was an extreme I'd never encountered. Twas a lesson I learned, that
I should ascertain some restraint, for when they take their own lives
or the lives of others, the fear dies with them. Without fear, I cannot
be and so I found that I could—and should—no longer push said
envelope to the brink of falling off the table. My own existence
depended upon it. Besides, extreme fear led to their madness. And
madness . . . well, madness makes fear eternal.

—From the diary of Tenebris, The Boogeyman

HERE IN AMERICA, we tend to be a little too realistic when it
comes to teaching our children the ins-and-outs of morality.

"If you do that, you'll never get into a good college" or "Don't do that
or you'll never be able to father children."

In Japan, however . . .

"If you do that, the Namahage will come down from their mountain
and take you away forever in their buckets" and "Don't do that or the
Kappa will drag you to your death in the river and eat you alive, slowly,
over the course of several days."

Sure, we have our own monsters here in the States, but the monsters
in Japan, China, Korea, and the Philippines are still looked upon as very
real threats to disobedient children and wayward adults. Legends, myths,

and stories of generally monstrous horrors still resonate there today as they did at the beginning of time. None were more terrifying the The Namahage (pronounced "Nom-a-hahg.")

Long before the birth of Christ, the Namahage roamed the mountains and hills of Japan's Oga region. From their hidden caves atop the Honzan and Shinzan mountain peaks, the Namahage would stalk the villages below at night, stealing rice crops and abducting beautiful young women to take with them back to their homes as slaves.

Fed up with the obstinate ogres, the citizens of Oga made a bet with the demons of Honzan and Shinzan. The

The Namahage were meant to be fearsome and terrifying. (*Artist unknown.*)

wager was simple: if the Namahage could build a flight of 1,000 steps that spanned from the village to the top of Shinzan in a single night, then the Namahage would willingly receive an offering of one woman a year picked by lottery by the villagers. But if they should fail in their task, then the Namahage would have to leave the area forever and never return.

The challenge was accepted and the Namahage readily agreed to the terms. They went to work, speedily crafting elegant stone steps as the villagers had asked. But before they were finished, a wily villager mimicked the crow of a rooster, which of course signified the end of night and the beginning of day. Believing they had failed, the Namahage retreated from the area, dishonored and ashamed of their failure. They left behind 999 perfectly crafted steps, one short of their goal. And on their mountains they stayed while their legend proliferated. The Namahage's propensity for stealing beautiful young women became a need to steal disobedient children of any age.

Like many demons of the age, the Namahage had many different levels of intimidation, ranging from the public shaming of cowards to brutal physical attacks on unsuspecting travelers. In truth, the stories of the Namahage influenced the very core of Japanese family values and the values placed on honor.

Though they're mostly seen as costumed men performing on the Oga Peninsula during the New Year's ritual, the Namahage and their fearsome scowls and outlandish appearances have changed little over their lifetime. Neither have their methods, as the costumed Namahage travel up and down the peninsula, going door-to-door, seeking out lazy, whiny children to take back to their mountain hideaways.

"Are there any crybabies around? Are naughty kids about?" they'll bellow as children cowered and cried. Parents fed up with insolent and recalcitrant children would often "feed" them to the Namahage, who would drag them out into the snow and roar incessantly into their faces until fear found them once more and the slate had been wiped clean for another year. The Namahage could be sated by offerings of food and sake before making their way on to the next home on the street. And as the dark night swallowed them, the children were once again reminded of why they must fear the night. While terror may have been the most obvious facet of the Namahage, the blessings bestowed upon the family following their visit ensured that the business of purging the wildness of the children had worked and that the year ahead would be full of promise and prosperity.

But if they weren't good, the Namahage *would* know, and they would return.

> Using their system of honor against them, I created a lasting fear that survived thousands of generations. It was a wellspring that rejuvenated itself every February during the Japanese New Year's festivities.
>
> —From the diary of Tenebris, The Boogeyman

THE KAPPA

The child was alone, which was a good thing for me. The less adults see of me, the better. Yet I did not strike. I watched the boy, who was only four, perhaps five years-old. He walked too close to the riverbank and I was seized by a remembrance of the Nøkken I had conjured in Norway in what seemed like so many millennia ago. When I closed my eyes and listened to his heart beat, I relished the quickening of it as the Kappa rose from the river and took him. But I did not allow the boy to die just yet, for the tale could not begin until he was witnessed in its clutches. And oh, was he witnessed, thrashing about in the clutches of a scaly beast as it dragged him beneath the water. And so, the Kappa was born.

— From the diary of Tenebris, The Boogeyman

THE JAPANESE CULTURE was born upon the backs of dragons, a beast that once numbered in the millions, that once dotted the skies like stars. Over time, the dragons were hunted and killed, their nests destroyed, and became all but extinct. Those who did not die evolved into reptiles and sea creatures, and though their sizes diminished, their pride remained enormous; they demanded respect but found little. Humans were their bane, and it angered the remaining dragons; certainly, dragons of old were revered, but the lizards and salamanders they had to become were not. Into hiding they went, disguising themselves in rivers, lakes, and oceans. They sought refuge in the earth and in dense jungles. One such creature was the Kappa, supposedly born from the memory of Tenebris as he re-imagined the Nøkken for the Asian culture. These near-mythic, yet very real, giant salamanders that inhabited the lakes, rivers, and swamps of Japan, crawled on all fours with bulbous heads, looking much like monstrous human-like creatures creeping through the mud and kelp of the waterways.

With webbed feet and a shiny, scaly coat that ranges from yellow to green, the Kappa have been sighted sporting a beak for a mouth and a shell across its body, which makes them resemble lizard-like turtles. Atop the head is a bald plate that serves as armor for the brain as well as a cap for the great powers of aquatic survival. It is said that if the cap were to crack, the Kappa's powers would diminish slowly before it died.

Perhaps even more terrifying than the appearance of the Kappa is what it does to you once it ensnares and drags you beneath the surface of the water. Wrestling you into submission, the Kappa will drink your blood and harvest your liver, sustaining its physical hunger before feeding its spiritual hunger on your shirkodama, a mythical ball of powerful human energy located conveniently in your anus. It will crawl up into you, devouring the shirkodama and everything else in its path as it eats you from the inside out.

Even more disturbing are the folk tales of Kappa raping human women washing clothes or bathing at the riverside. Pulled screaming into the water, the Kappa violates the woman and sets her free, impregnated by a repulsive offspring that was often buried alive upon its birth. This scene was recorded by Kunio Yanaugita, an early twentieth-century folklorist, who wrote of the Kappa in his seminal work on Japan's rich folklore, 1908's Tono Monogatari.

Taking flight from a Kappa was almost always a futile endeavor, though there were a few tricks one could employ to safely escape one. Being Japanese and obsessed with politeness, if one were to bow to the Kappa, he would be bound to return the bow, making it possible for one to run off to safety. Challenging the Kappa to a physical match of strength was another diversion, usually leading to Sumo-type wrestling; defeat renders the Kappa impotent and it slinks away in defeat. And if that doesn't work, try dousing it with iron, sesame, or ginger. It hates that.

But not every Kappa is out to devour the human race. Some humans have been able to befriend the creatures, bribing them with eggplant, noodles, or cucumbers—foods they enjoy more than the flesh of children.

The Japanese Kappa bears a striking resemblance in body and spirit to the Vodyanoy, a Slavic water sprite, making a case for the proliferation of water beasts and sprites around the world that are connected by similar genetic traits. (*Illustration by Ivan Bilbin, 1934.*)

In fact, the Kappa like cucumbers so much that there is even a type of cucumber sushi roll known as Kappamaki.

As time rolled on and the legend of the Kappa softened in Tenebris's absence, Kappa became known for helping farmers tend to the fields and flocks, and aiding with medicines and healing

> I had nothing to do with that. When left alone for too long, your children tend to go their own way. I did not approve of Kappa aiding the humans, but I had other fish to fry, so to speak. I understand their need to fit in, though I find it difficult to condone. Ah well, you cannot win them all.
>
> —Tenebris, The Boogeyman, (Interview #2, 11/8/2015)

KOREA'S DOKKAIBI

BY HIS OWN admission, the Dokkaibi was Tenebris's imagination let loose with its guard down. Though frightening, it was also a playful goblin-like creature that sought out the friendship and games of humans with which he could play. It could honestly be said that the Dokkaibi was The Boogeyman's attempt at being benevolent, though this was a phase that—blessedly—did not last long.

Resembling a Nordic troll, but retaining the size of a goblin or sprite, the Dokkaibi would go on to appear in numerous Korean folktales, usually portrayed as mischievous creatures who enjoyed playing tricks on villains and other mean people. One example comes from the story of an old man who once lived alone on a high mountain peak. One day, he was visited by the Dokkaibi, and to the surprise of the Dokkaibi, the old man was very kind and accepted him into his home, languishing his guest with food and drink. The two quickly became friends. Day after day, the old man and the Dokkaibi spent time together, talking and walking through the mountains and the surrounding forests. But one day, the old man was alone near a mountain stream when he caught his reflection in the glistening water. It turns out that he was beginning to resemble the Dokkaibi, and he immediately feared that he himself was becoming a Dokkaibi after spending so much time with his new, but monstrous, friend. When the Dokkaibi returned, the old man asked his friend, "What are you most afraid of?" and the Dokkaibi answered, "I'm afraid of blood. What are you afraid of?"

The old man shrugged and a shiver could be seen running down his spine. "I'm afraid of money, my friend. That is why I live here alone. Away from the greed and temptation money brings." The very next day, the old man killed his prize cow and poured the blood all over his house. Shocked and filled with great anger, the Dokkaibi ran off. "I shall return with *your* greatest fear, old man!" he bellowed, and return he did. The next day, he piled huge bags of money, silver, and gold around the old man's house. Feeling that they were now even, the Dokkaibi walked away in victory never to return. However, the old man soon became known as the richest man in the region.

In some cases, however, their demeanor and method of operating resembles that of a Celtic troll, challenging travelers in its forest to wrestling matches for the right to pass without harm. Carrying a mallet-like club called a bangmang, the Dokkaibi uses it to summon whatever it wants. Much like a magic wand, the bangmang cannot create out of thin air, but summons the object by stealing it from someone else, which is why the Dokkaibi is also blamed for things disappearing around the house.

In creating the Dokkaibi, Tenebris laid out a number of different, very specialized goblins, all with a singular purpose but with differing means to the end. In all, the Dokkaibi were meant to hassle mankind incessantly but were created to go about it in different ways. For example, the Cham Dokkaibi was the classic mischievous Dokkaibi, whereas the Gae Dokkaibi was capable only of pure evil, and what it did to punish villagers and traveler's bordered on the grotesque. Entire herds of cattle could be dismembered overnight, or children could be stolen from their beds without warning. The Gim Dokkaibi were more like trolls, dull headed and with an agricultural leaning, unlike the Gaksi, female Dokkaibi who used their feminine wiles and keen intelligence to deceive human men.

CHINA'S MOGWAI

Spielberg still owes me money for that one.
— Tenebris, The Boogeyman, (Interview #2, 11/08/2015)

IN 1984'S *GREMLINS*, a small New England town is besieged by monstrous little creatures run amok because of the American's lack of responsibility in taking care of a mythological Chinese animal known as Mogwai. What most people tend to overlook is the fact that Mogwai were real and that they were quite the thorn in China's side during the medieval era.

Derived from the Sanskrit word for "evil beings," the Mogwai initially meddled in the fates of all Hindus and Buddhists, leading them into trouble, sin, temptation, and self-destruction, causing the pious to be caught up in a never-ending cycle of reincarnation and eternal damnation. Little demons, these guys. Eventually, the story of the Mogwai evolved into a sort of ghost story as the diminutive creatures became evil spirits capable of demonic possession, torment, and unholy vengeance upon those who still lived.

But the legend of the Mogwai as a disruptive little creature made its way out of China and into British and American folklore, most notoriously with the beginnings of World War II. While the Mogwai are rooted firmly in Chinese folklore, the term "Gremlin" is uniquely Celtic, derived from the old English word *gremian*, which means "to vex." Author Carol Rose even went so far as to say the word "gremlin" came about by combining the Grimm's Fairy Tales with Fremlin Beer. With Celtic folklore, in contrast to the Chinese legends, the Gremlins were more like fairy tale dwarfs, handy with tools and with a good work ethic. They were also very willing to please their human counterparts, but most believe that they turned against the humans when they were denied recognition for their formidable efforts. The Gremlins became devious creatures out to sabotage Allied planes, tanks, and other very necessary tools of war. Though the Gremlins could undermine any piece of technology, they seemed to hold a special interest in aviation and pilots and crew aboard these Allied planes often resorted to blaming Gremlins when something would go wrong with the machinery.

> The old Royal Naval Air Service in 1917 and the newly constituted Royal Air Force in 1918 appear to have detected the existence of a horde of mysterious and malicious sprites whose whole purpose in life was . . . to bring about as many as possible of the inexplicable mishaps which, in those days as now, trouble an airman's life.
>
> —Britain's *The Spectator* newspaper, 1918

A British sign, usually placed in munitions and aircraft factories during World War I, warned workers of the exploits of "gremlins" and their devious mission to undermine the Allied forces. (*Artist unknown.*)

Oddly enough, the Gremlin plight was taken very seriously by the British Air Ministry, which appointed Pilot Officer Percy Prune to write a service manual detailing their exploits and offering ways to either get rid of them or at least placate them until the mission could be completed without any major mishap. And whereas the United States had begun Project Blue Book in an effort to study Unidentified Flying Objects, the British established "Project Green Book," which studied anomalies where the cause was undetermined. But Project Green Book was hardly taken seriously, even by the military itself; personnel were ordered to disregard talk of Gremlins and any conversation regarding Gremlins was seen to be unprofessional.

THE ASWANG
AND MANANANGGAL

I have a mean streak within me an eternity long. I have no issues
with taking life as long as the fear it creates makes up for the loss
ten-fold. As time went on, I grew tired of playing with humans. I
was no longer content with scaring them. The spilling of blood and
the lakes it created harbored luscious fear in others and I grew to
enjoy the ripping of flesh and the guttural screams that came as a
result.

—From the diary of Tenebris, The Boogeyman

IN APPEARANCE, THE Aswang of the Philippines very much
resembled the classic vampire of Germanic and Romanian folklore,
but it was Tenebris's intention from the start to craft the Aswang as more
ghoulish, unrepentant, and downright nasty. Having had his fill of polite
monsters and genial creatures, Tenebris let loose the chains and went
straight for the throat when he arrived in the Philippines—more specifically
the island of Capiz. Early in the sixteenth century, Tenebris had stowed
away in the shadowy holds of Japanese ships and stepped foot upon the
beaches of the Philippines for the first time. With a population comprised
of equal parts native islanders, Japanese immigrants, and French and
Spanish tradesmen, the air was ripe for the breeding of serious monsters.

Very soon after his arrival, villagers began to tell stories of terrifying
beasts stalking the night—tales of unusually large cats, dogs, and boars
tramping through shadows and brush seeking out raw flesh to eat. It was
speculated, but never proven, that these beasts were human during the
day, living silently as reclusive hermits until the sun dropped and the
moon rose. Then, transforming, the Aswang would go in search of flesh
and blood.

In their hungry form, the Aswang are emaciated and gangley with
mottled skin and milky eyes, and despite their tattered appearance, the
Aswangs are terrifyingly fast and athletic creatures, jumping up to twenty feet into the air and pouncing on their fleeing prey. Despite their
rotted appearance and odor, the Aswang are incredibly athletic, having
the ability to run at phenomenal speeds, as they pursue their terrified
soon-to-be victims and dinner combined. No wonder that the zombie-vam-
pire legends have taken such a firm hold.

Small children began to disappear from their homes in the dead of
night. Pregnant women would wake to find their unborn children half-eat-
en at their feet; many believe that the long snout of the Aswang would
worm into the womb of the woman and pull the fetus out with its long,

jagged tongue, eating its fill silently and leaving the ruined corpse behind as a sign of its presence.

As villagers began to learn more about their foe, the Aswang's nature became more common knowledge. For instance, it would often throw its voice, sounding as if it were miles away when it was in fact only a few feet behind you, a tactic meant to lull their victim into a false sense of security. In addition to its bloodcurdling ventriloquism skills, the Aswang would often change forms during pursuits, truly throwing off their would-be captors.

When live prey could not be found, the Aswang resorted to stealing fresh corpses from in-home wakes, leaving tree trunks or banana leaves in place of the dearly departed. In the times before chemical preservation, it was a quick way to scavenge a meal for the night.

But at the end of the night when the hunt is over and its hunger is sated, the Aswang will return to its human form, easing back into a suspicious society but looking quite hung over, either from having been up all night or from becoming thoroughly blood drunk. As humans, Aswangs had been known to marry humans with the result being an inability to reproduce and the significant other becoming Aswang as well. If this does happen, the two married Aswangs will hunt together but go off in different directions. While they resemble boars or dogs and appear to be pack-like creatures, it became well known very quickly that hungry Aswangs rarely like to share their meals.

From a behavioral point of view, the Aswang is very much an honor killer, opting to search well outside of their home villages for food. "Striking at home," Tenebris told me, "would rally suspicion within a night." Therefore, the Aswang pursues its prey in far-off hunting grounds.

But being the polite yet vicious killer it is doesn't exempt the Aswang from persecution. It is destroyed as soon as it is discovered, killed at a barong barong, a hastily made shanty cabin that is immediately torn down and rebuilt elsewhere so that the spirit of the Aswang cannot linger at the place of its death, haunting it and its residents until doomsday. Destruction of the Aswang comes at the business end of many different objects, the most popular being a whip made from the tail of a stingray. But when in doubt, decapitation is almost always effective as a means to an end for the little beast.

With the Aswang, Tenebris let loose upon the islanders a whole new idea of fear and absolute horror. The older natives still speak of their encounters with the Aswang to this day, while younger citizens report more encounters with the fearsome creature than ever before, and as time goes on, different species of Aswangs have come to the forefront, including the wolf-like Sigbin, the ghoulish phantasm Berberoka, and the monkey-like BalBal. The name "Aswang" began to be seen as a generic term for the various types of blood-drinking monsters plaguing the Filipino people.

For Tenebris, "It was exhilarating to dream up such a foul creature and watch it flourish as it did, becoming more horrific with each evolution, for I had watched horror become soft so often in the Nordic and Celtic lands. It was nice to see horror germinate and flower so nastily into these other creatures. Like having step-children, only not as horrible or as taxing emotionally."

But Tenebris was hardly finished with the Filipino men and women. Not by a long shot. Driven by the success of his Aswang, Tenebris created the absurdly horrific and downright terrifying Manananggal, a female Aswang who ate human flesh and drank human blood. Often seen as a witch-like creature with long jagged teeth and white eyes, the Manananggal was capable of severing its upper torso and sprouting leathery wings, leaving its legs behind as it flew away in search of prey, which, like the Aswang, consisted of unborn children and sleeping men and women. Children were not exempt from the Manananggal, either. Black cats and crows seemed to signal the presence of the Manananggal, while facial deformations in babies was blamed on botched Manananggal attacks.

If one were to come across the legs of the Manananggal, a sprinkling of Holy salt upon the stumps would effectively spell out a death sentence for the Manananggal, for it would not be able to reunite with its legs where Holy salt had been lain. Unable to return to its "human" form, the Manananggal would succumb to the sunrise and be destroyed.

Which led to my next question: If you are creating these beasts, why give them a weakness such as herbs, or sunlight, or silver? To which Tenebris, smiling softly, leaned in, and whispered: "The illusion of hope breeds fear as much as it breeds resilience. What fear is left when hope disappears? No hope equals no fear, my friend. Don't forget the business I am in."

CHAPTER FIVE

THE WORST OF THEM ALL

CHILD CATCHERS, CHANGELINGS, AND CANNIBALS

> What delectable fear it is that comes from the tears of parents when their child is stolen. What horrors awaited their precious little children? Each nightmare was different, and with each one came a new opportunity to plumb the depths of madness and terror. I planted the seed, but the weed grew too fast and destroyed the garden I envisioned. Today, nothing but vipers live among those tall grasses and even I fear to tread inside of it.
>
> —From the diary of Tenebris, The Boogeyman

THE MOST DELICIOUSLY memorable character in Roald Dahl's adaptation of Ian Fleming's *Chitty Chitty Bang Bang* is known only as The Child Catcher. He is a diabolical, black-maned hunter of children who works for Baron and Baroness Bomburst, rulers of Vulgaria. Never featured in the original novel, The Child Catcher is a thing of pure, vile villainy, using the mantra of "Lollipops! Free Lollipops today!" to lure children into the streets so he can cage them for a trip to the Vulgarian dungeons, all because Baroness Bomburst despises them.

While The Child Catcher is one brilliant writer's creation, it is still every parent's worst nightmare: the notion that a complete stranger will lie to and manipulate their children into leaving with them, and what's worse are the thoughts of what would happen to those children once the monster had them all to himself. Even if you're not a parent, the terror of children facing unimaginable horror without protection is almost too much to bear, and while every area of the world has its own version of a "Sack Man" or "Child Stealer," each one is defined by its own culture, adding things here and there that reflect the preeminent social mores of the time. Child abductions and murders are sadly so common in this day and age, so common, in fact that these next few monsters are seen as oddly refreshing and blissfully antiquated. It is with these creatures and figures that parents tend to threaten their children with, punished for doing bad things by remorseless monsters like The Sack Man, El Cucuy, and even Santa Claus himself (He *does* see you when you're sleeping, *and* he *knows* when you're awake, after all). These tales of monsters stealing children and doing things with—and to—them are timeless and terrifying yet still manage to leave a lingering hope in their wakes.

THE SACK MAN

OF COURSE, THE tales all begin with the infamous Sack Man, a shadowy figure that stalks through the village with a sack over his shoulder, looking for children out past their bedtime. Once he finds you, he stuffs you into his bag and carries you off into the night, never to be seen or heard from again. The legend of the Sack Man reminds us of prior folktales, such as the Baba Yaga and the Namahage, and he is definitely within that same wheel house. Where the Sack Man differs is that there is no escape from the horror he has in mind, nor can there be a bargain brokered. He simply is evil, and his hungers are exotic to say the least. While there are certainly a large number of boogeymen who carry a sack or container to hold their stolen children, the Sack Man is different in that, in nearly every culture, the description of him is the same. Described as skeletal, gangly, and creepy, this disturbing humanoid-type creature carries his thick burlap bag over his shoulder, oftentimes wearing a similar sack over his head as a disguise. He dresses in rags similar to ones worn by old-time tramps and peasants who scavenged their clothing from the dead. One trait that always seems to follow the Sack Man around is the intensity of his stare, almost as if he can paralyze you with a glance. Some believers in the United Kingdom say his eyes are piercing blue, while those in Europe and Asia claim they are all white with only black pinpricks of pupils visible. Still others, like those in Mexico, Spain, and Brazil, claim that the Sack Man has no eyes, but yet can still dig deep into your soul.

The Sack Man of Mexico and Spain, known collectively as El Cucuy, is perhaps one of the best-known tales of a roving wanderer who steals children. Known also as the Coco (a name he garnered for the rough, coconut-like texture of his skin), El Cucuy is usually mentioned as a warning by the parents of disobedient children. Lullabies and rhymes sung to their children at night tended to nail down the importance of compliance, for if they were not, El Cucuy would get them. He will take the form of shadows along the rooftops, always vigilant, always looking for children to steal and feast upon. Making himself known to the children, they will see a horrific, demonic-looking creature with rough skin and wiry hair. He will wear a cloak that is either black or dark gray and he will sometimes be carrying his large burlap sack with him. El Cucuy's legacy has

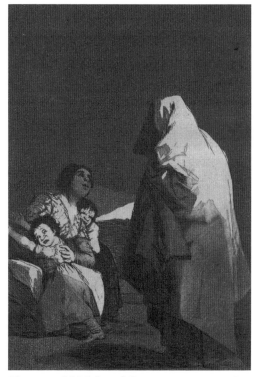

The most faithful, and famous, representation of El Cucuy, sketched by Francisco Goya in 1799.

spread over much of the Spanish- and Portuguese-speaking world, such as the Portuguese Homem do Saco and Spain's El Hombre del Costa. All are names that are roughly translated as "man with a sack." All look and act the same with little to no deviation in the myth.

In Scotland, the Sack Man is referred to as a Lammikin, a demonic creature that stabs and bites young and infant children in order to waken their mothers. While the blood of children is divine, the blood of the mother is even better, and the wail of her children brings her to him quicker. But the Lammikin is sort of an anomaly in the Child Eater/Stealer category: he draws blood because of a thirst for it. The true nature of the child stealer, and the main emphasis for its life, is punishment for uncontrolled behavior. Eating the child is a secondary motive. In this case, I guess you could say he is fairly biased, and his prey has to fall into a certain bracket to be considered.

CHANGELINGS

A SLIGHT DEVIATION OF the Sack Man myth, the lore concerning Changelings turns the legend back to a more supernatural realm. In the old days, evil or mischievous faeries and demons would steal newborn babies from their cribs and replace them with demonic doppelgangers. Faeries have long been known to steal human children and substitute changelings: faerie babies or sometimes just a piece of wood that seems to be alive for a short time. The Welsh sometimes refer to these fairies as "cipenapers," a progenitor of the word "kidnapper." According to most stories in the folktale canons, pretty young women, unbaptized babies, and blonde children ran the greatest risk of being Faerie-napped, but pretty much anyone who wandered too close to known faerie mounds at night took their lives in their own hands. While the Changeling will almost always resemble a human child, it will transform and show its faerie side eventually, looking older quicker, perhaps more wizened or elderly. A deformity may occur, or they may show a tremendous fondness for dancing and eating. The left-handed children of Ireland are all considered to be Changelings, but that may be taking the folktale a bit too far.

The Changelings would almost always be found out, for a mother knows her child inside and out above all other things in the world, and when something doesn't seem normal, a mother will know it. When the Changeling is discovered, it will fly up the chimney or out the nearest window, returning the missing child in its wake.

Similarly, the Trows of the Shetland Islands near the coast of Scotland will leave a very gnarly, sickly looking Changeling in the place of the baby it's just stolen. Unlike the Faerie Changelings, it's fairly obvious from the start that it is not a human child. The trows are simply lazy that way, and they don't seem to care much if they're found out. Trows are notorious night creepers, known for their misshapen bodies and heads, sunken eyes and wild-ling hair. Dressing in gray rags to blend into the Scottish mists, their diminutive size likens them to elves or gremlins, but that is as close to those other, tamer creatures as they get. Not known for their understanding or benevolence, the Trows can hold a grudge forever if they feel they have been offended, such as what happened in the case of one Scottish family who forgot how much the trow liked to warm themselves by their fire. Before going to bed one night, this family locked their doors and windows and in doing so, kept the trow from entering to enjoy the roaring fireplace. To say the trow were upset is definitely an understatement, as this particular family endured a pestilence-like curse courtesy of the trow for many years before it suddenly abated. People on the island mostly keep their doors unlocked nowadays to avoid angering the trows.

However . . .

Not all trows want to merely warm themselves by your fire. They wouldn't be included here if that was the worst they could do. Most of them want to take advantage of your hospitable nature to steal your children. Legend has it that a fisherman once saw a pack of trows running along the dark moonlit path leading up to his brother-in-law's house where his little sister lay in her bed. Running ahead of them to the front door, the fisherman turned the key in the iron lock, refusing the trow entry. Furious, the trow placed a curse on the fisherman, stealing his ability to move in any way. For hours and hours, the fisherman stood outside the house, his hand on the locked door and the key inside the lock, unable to move. Finally, an old woman passed by and blessed him, releasing him from the curse of the trows.

WHEN IN ROME . . . OR GREECE . . .

OF COURSE, WHEN it comes to child eaters and kidnappers, no one holds a candle to the Greeks and the mythology of Middle Eastern countries. One of the main staples of Greek mythology is the story of Kronos, the original father of the world and one of the first Titans who decided to devour his children to keep them from taking his throne away from him. Then there is the story of Tantalus, who killed and cooked his own son, Pelops, and served him to the gods in an effort to find out if the gods really did know all that was going on in the world. Of course, the gods found out, Pelops was resurrected, and Tantalus was sent to Tartarus, the deepest, darkest pit of the Underworld reserved exclusively for the punishment of the worst sinners imaginable. While in Tartarus, Tantalus was forced to stand in a deep pool of water, his head just barely breaking the surface, with luscious apples hanging from a branch above him. But whenever Tantalus reached for the branch, the branch itself would pull away, keeping the fruit from his grasping hand. This was how the word "tantalize" came to be in the English language, describing perfectly the tantalizing fruit that is always out of reach. Similarly, the tale of Lycaeon had this semi-famous Greek pulling the same stunt, though when Zeus found out, he punished him by murdering the rest of Lycaeon's sons, fifty in all.

Then there was the tragic tale of Lamia, one of Zeus's mistresses and a queen of Libyan descent. As Zeus and Lamia carried on their illicit affair, Zeus's wife, Hera (who was never good at tolerating her husband's affairs), exacted a terrible revenge. Hera murdered each and every one of Lamia's children, then turned the mistress into a horrific demon whose sole purpose was to hunt down and murder innocent children. It was also said that Hera cursed Lamia with the inability to close her eyes so that she would always obsess over the images of the children she had killed and eaten. But Zeus took pity on Lamia and granted her the power to remove her eyes so that she might be granted *some* peace. What a nice guy, though he never seemed to mind when his mistresses were reprimanded by Hera, and he rarely (if ever) stepped in to aid them. Even as the ruler of the gods, Zeus knew better than to meddle in the dealings of a scorned woman.

The Greek gods didn't fool around, and their favorite punishments were exactly what people who tell stories of the child eaters are afraid of: losing their children in a maelstrom of absolute horror that is both insane and grisly. But Greece and Rome don't hold a monopoly on demonic or ill-tempered deities. Between

Saturn Devouring His Children (1819–1823) by Francisco Goya.

the lands of Sumeria, Zoroastria, and Babylon, and huddled deep in the realms of Satanism, Christianity, Islam, and Buddhism, there are no ends to the numbers of demons who prey on children, and they all serve the same purpose of the non-secular folktales: to scare the daylights out of little children and make them behave before their God. Such religious extremism isn't new and it certainly still takes place today.

BLOOD LIBEL

T HE IDEA OF spilling the blood of children took on a horrific and very real turn when anti-Semites in the Middle East began what is now called a "Blood libel," which is, simply, accusing the Jewish people of murdering children for their religious rituals. While it seems laughable and farfetched now, this was a very serious accusation that began as far back as 356 BCE when Haman attempted to murder the entire tribe of Abraham. According to the Book of Esther of the Old Testament, Haman attempted to stage the genocide of the Jews in Persia by proclaiming them to be murderers of children. But his plot was foiled by Queen Esther, who herself was a Jew. Haman was hanged alongside the bodies of his ten sons, who had been killed in battle fighting the Jewish people. The "Blood Libel" would continue on for centuries, culminating with the hate crimes perpetrated by Adolf Hitler and his Nazi party, who regularly used Blood Libel as a means for promoting their own brand of genocidal anti-Semitism.

Tragically, in more recent times, the terrorist group ISIS out of Syria, has been reported to have served human flesh to their captives, killed and cooked into stews and fillets. One story that has circled about for a while is the tale of a Kurdish woman whose son had been kidnapped by ISIS. When the woman went to meet with them to negotiate his safe return, they welcomed her with cups of tea, and a meal of meat, rice, and soup. After she had finished eating, she asked to see her son. "You've just eaten him," they told her, laughing as she wept and screamed in horror.

Sometimes, even humans can outdo demons.

CHAPTER SIX

ALL THINGS CONNECT

NATIVE AMERICAN TERRORS

One of the more intriguing aspects of my job is improvisation. Working with the environment you are in to create something inspired. With the native people of the United States, I could easily harvest fear from the glance of a doe in the darkest night, or even the presence of a wolf where there should be none. The native terrors that bred and spread across the lands still hold to this day, and some are hard to deny. The horror is still a part of them and always will be. Human life is but one thread in a loom, and in the loom, all things connect. Monsters included.

—From the diary of Tenebris, The Boogeyman

IN THE EARLIEST years of the New World's discovery, along with the natural unrest of the native people, monsters were bred, born, raised, and set loose upon the undiscovered wilderness. The early settlers and immigrants brought fear of the new lands with them and their fears were not quelled by the dense forests surrounding what would become known as America. The native people, having lived there for generations, had their own religions, their own gods, their own devils, and the Europeans stepped into that maelstrom rather unwittingly. Convinced that they could convert the "heathens," the Europeans were easily taken in by the demons and monsters conjured to frighten them off. But rather than spook them, the Europeans found their suspicions confirmed, and it was only a matter of time before the natives would be fighting for not only their freedom, but their very lives.

83

Into the fray came Tenebris, whispering into the ears of the shamans and chiefs, aiding them in conjuring guardians that would protect the land and the people who held it sacred. Tenebris, whether he chose to admit it or not, saw the threat of the Europeans as dangerously real. It would be as if he could see the future, and it was a mere shade of what the natives had hoped for the younger generations. Borrowing liberally from his creations across the Atlantic and infusing them with the fiery blood of the Native Americans, Tenebris helped to produce iconic monstrosities and protectors whose fearsome reputations would persevere well into the future and be held in high esteem to this day.

But it wasn't just for the benefit of the natives that Tenebris performed his work. He truly had an interest in creating new nightmares for this New World and the deal with the natives was only the beginning. Soon, tales of monsters, witches, ghosts, and demons would spread across the original colonies and into the vast wonderland of dark forests, desolate plains, and impenetrable mountains. The work of Tenebris, The Boogeyman, in America was a new level of genius, completely original to the New World while still casting a shadow that had first been thrown thousands of years before across Europe.

THE WINDIGO

IN THE DARK, snow-capped mountains and hills of Canada and the Northern United States, it walks amid the sparkling frost and sub-zero temperatures. Finding camouflage among the thick trees and foliage, the great beast stalks its prey. Just ahead, it can see the glow of fire and the silhouette of make-shift tents. A slight murmuring of human voices. Slightly erratic, nervous heartbeats. As it moves silently from its hiding spot closer to the humans, it gently rubs its antlers against tree branches overhead and it pauses. The humans heard it. The clicking of rifles cocking. Poised and ready to strike, it lunges and feels the blood in its mouth almost immediately.

The Windigo is coming and you are on its list.

Before the night is over, another three are dead, devoured, and destined to become another tale in the legend of the Windigo, the most fearsome legend in Native American folklore. Believed to be both human and demi-god, the Windigo's reputation is equal parts sheer terror and morality tale run amok. Feared by Algonquin peoples across the Northern United States and portions of Canada, the Windigo legend came about out of the fears of cannibalism during the harshest of winters. The Algonquin and Potawatomi believed that a human man can become the

Windigo after he eats the flesh of another human, while Chippewa and Ottawa peoples believed the Windigo was a very real beast that stalked the wintry landscape in search of stranded travelers or settlers to devour.

Described as having the upper body of a man and the cloven hooves of a stag, the Windigo was primarily known for the incredible rack of antlers protruding from its head. Emaciated and gaunt, the Windigo's skin was gray and clung tightly to its bones, its eyes sunken and emotionless. A glaze of ice covers its body and the head of the human it once was protrudes from where its heart ought to be, its terrorized expression frozen in time. An odor of death and decay followed after it, poisoning the air with its pungent scent of corrupted flesh. Those who become Windigo will only find escape in the arms of death.

The topic of cannibalism is a taboo subject, not only to the civilized world, but also to the native people, for cannibalism, even to save ones own life, was seen as a dishonorable, devilish act. In the case of famine, most believed that suicide or starving to death was preferable to eating your dead buddy, and anyone who did would become a Windigo themselves. That's not to say that cannibalism wasn't practiced. The tragedy of the Donner Party of 1847 is a prime example where settlers traveling to California got stranded in the Sierra Nevada mountains during one of the most brutal winters on record. They too resorted to cannibalism, and while their determination to live is down-played, their grisly means of survival is the only thing people tend to remember. So, in essence, the Donner Party too became Windigo, forever associated with the eating of human flesh. Unlike the newly arrived Europeans who took everything at face value, The Natives saw no division between humans and beasts, judging people based on their actions and the intent in their heart, for truly, that is where the beast sleeps and wakes.

Such was the case of the bizarre Old West tracker, Alferd Packer, who became stranded with his party near Breckenridge, Colorado, in 1874. But in Packer's case, not only did he eat his human companions, he didn't even wait for nature to kill them, opting to do the job himself with a hatchet. Packer proclaimed his innocence until the very end, saying that it was another one of the hunters whom he had killed in self defense. But it did little good, for he received a conviction for manslaughter and was sentenced to forty years in a frontier prison, of which he only served seventeen. Archaeologists and museum authorities in Colorado would later recover a gun Packer claimed to have used as well. Using modern forensic technology, combined with the evidence they already had, they seemed to prove Packer's innocence. Alferd Packer's story, infused tightly with the Windigo legend, would eventually inspire new variations on the Windigo legend, culminating with 1999's ultra-black comedy period film *Ravenous* and Trey Parker's cult classic *Cannibal! The Musical.*

While some of the cultures differed on where the Windigo came from, whether it was a divine creation or the creation of man's gluttony and greed, it is a fairly common belief that humans can easily turn into Windigos either by resorting to cannibalism or by becoming possessed by the spirit of the Windigo, an act which normally occurred in dreams and nightmares. A punishment for lowering oneself to feast on human flesh, becoming the Windigo meant that this human would forever stalk human prey with a hunger that would never be satisfied and would constantly grow and grow.

As interest in the paranormal reaches critical mass in this new age, it is hardly surprising that a spotlight is being shone on cryptozoology, more specifically, the legend of the Windigo as it pertains to the legend of Bigfoot. It isn't hard to believe that the legend of the Windigo arose from the numerous sightings of the creature known today as Sasquatch or Bigfoot. Tacking on a moral to the story, much like many folktales, gave the creature purpose in a world that seemed delicately random to many. It was also a fairly handy method of connecting the dots for Bigfoot trackers and folklore enthusiasts alike. We'll get into the Bigfoot and Sasquatch legends later.

Aside from the classic attributes of a Windigo, it was also said to have had a special relationship with water and more specifically to ice. Some cultures closer to the glacial streams, rivers, and lakes of the North believed that the Windigo was either formed from glacial ice or shared a symbiotic relationship with it of some sort. Take the story of the newlywed couple and the Windigo, a classic tale from numerous woodland Indian tribes. The tale revolves around a newlywed couple who moved close to the hunting grounds, where a child was soon born to them. As they looked in on him in his cradle, the newborn child spoke, asking them, "Where is that Sky Spirit? They say he is very powerful and some day I am going to meet him." Surprised that their baby was not only talking but forming complete, vocabulary-rich sentences, the mother told her child, "You should not talk about that Manido (spirit) that way."

Several nights later, the couple found their baby gone. A trail of baby feet in the snow led them toward a nearby lake, but soon, the feet became larger and looked almost like cloven hooves. Their baby had transformed into a Windigo, a voracious man-eater that would be feared forever. When they reached the lake, they saw the Windigo, surrounded by smaller, vicious, canine-looking minions that would protect it. But one of the minions threw a bolt of lightning at the Windigo, transforming him into a huge block of ice before he'd even hit the ground. Villagers from the area, who had been wakened by the sound of the Windigo, began to chop up the block of ice and melted the pieces. In the middle of the ice was the newlywed's baby, a hole in its head from where the lightning had struck him. Had the minion not killed the Windigo, it surely would have consumed the entire village.

In the canon of Windigo lore, there even exists the belief in Windigo hunters, with Ojibwa Indian Jack Fiddler being at the forefront of this short list of successful hunters. Hailing from Manitoba, Canada, Fiddler was a shaman for the Ojibwa tribe and the chief of the Sucker tribe of Sandy Lake, Manitoba. Like his father before him, Jack was renowned for conjuring spirits, casting spells, and aiding in helping the old and the sick. His experience with the Windigo became a personal mission when his own brother, Peter Flett, became one of the creatures during an especially treacherous trading expedition when he resorted to cannibalism to survive after rations ran out. Peter ultimately asked to be killed, a deed that Fiddler accepted and committed. With a body count of at least fourteen Windigo, Jack Fiddler was highly sought after by the tribes of his area, though his life's pursuit wasn't without its black marks. In early 1907, Fiddler and his son, Joseph, were arrested and tried for the murder of a Cree woman they claimed was a Windigo. Jack Fiddler escaped from the prison camp, and on September 30, 1907, he hung himself from a tree using his traditional sash as a slipknot noose.

The trial against Joseph Fiddler continued unabated, however, and the younger Fiddler was found guilty. Sentenced to death, he sadly passed on due to consumption three days before receiving news that his sentence would be overturned.

Following his arrest and prior to his suicide, Jack Fiddler was eulogized in a way by Methodist minister Joseph Albert George Lousley, who said, "He has not the slightest sign of enmity or hatred towards men nor God, no rebellion or unbelief, he is a quiet dignified man who has lived his life with a clear conscience."

THE DEER-WOMAN

THE DEER-WOMAN legend should be proof that the dangerous allure of mysterious, beautiful women alone in the forest isn't just a Celtic or Nordic tradition, nor is the notion that the animal world and the human world mingling together too fantastic to believe. Besides the natural danger of women in general, the Deer-Woman looks to ensnare unwary travelers in the forest, like the myth of man-stealing Mermaids and the portent of death herself, the Banshee. It's a familiar tale, but one that seems to exist in a time concurrent with those other tales of Celtic and Nordic beasties. One has to wonder, with the language barrier and the thousands of miles separating the continents, how did the stories come together and bear such a striking resemblance?

I could go on and on about land bridges connecting Siberia and Alaska, allowing people from different countries to come and go quite frequently before it was swallowed up by the Bering Sea. But the real truth is that the stories were spread by the same storyteller: Tenebris himself, a fact he passed on to me with a clearing of the throat and a well-timed nudge.

> The Deer-Woman was modeled after someone I knew a long, long time ago. A young girl I saw in one of the markets of Persia. She looked lost, troubled. Until I watched her mug and rob a 400-pound landowner and his man servant like it was nothing. Nothing! She was a wolf in lamb's clothing, and I thought, 'What a brilliant disguise.' It was not until much later that I realized that it was no disguise, but a defense mechanism. Also, going back to the idea of improvisation in your surroundings, I wanted her to be at one with the forest. That is how the Deer-Woman came about...
> — From the diary of Tenebris, The Boogeyman

While the origins of the Deer-Woman are fairly straightforward if Tenebris is to be believed, Potawatomi, Creek, Omaha, and Ponca Indian tribes believe she is the spirit of a native girl who was raped in the forest and transformed by the Great Spirit into the vengeful Deer-Woman to exact revenge upon girl-crazy men and boys.

Other legends say that Deer-Woman was a citizen of the forest, much like the Fauns of old faerie tales. Beautiful, alluring, and enchanting, Deer-Woman has the lower body and the deep brown eyes of a deer. Often seen hiding among the brush, trees, and greenery of the forest, she seeks out men to trap and keep with her forever. Sometimes, she will sing a haunting carol, or might even softly call the name of the man she wants in order to get his attention, always hiding the part of herself that is overtly animal. But once her prey is in reach, it is too late. The Deer-Woman has him and very few things can be done to escape. But there are a few tricks, such as pointing out her deer legs and hooves, which make her self-conscious, causing her to flee in shame. But not locking eyes with the Deer-Woman is the most powerful antidote for her enchantments. Unlike other beasts of enchantment, the Deer-Woman relies on the powerful connection she feels with her prey, exuding magic from her eyes.

Many stories abound about Deer-Woman, but my favorite tale revolves around a man in love with two women. These two women always attended the dances around the fire at night, but they always seemed to disappear right after without a trace. Intrigued, the young man tied a string to one of their dresses and held onto the string once the dances had stopped. He followed them until they both noticed and asked him what he wanted. "I want to go with you," he said. One of the women said, "All right. Near our home there is a big hole. We are going to jump into it and you jump in with us." When they got to the hole, the three jumped in, finding themselves in a large, dark cavern. Great numbers of deer were milling about and they all seemed to stare at the young man who obviously had no business being there. He was approached by three old Bucks who asked him what he was doing there.

"I came because I wanted to marry these women," he told the Bucks.

"Well, wait and it will soon be time to go out. When that time comes, they will go out, and you can have the women."

So the man waits and waits, and when it is finally time, he sees that the women he wants to marry had transformed into two beautiful does. Covering him with deer skin, the Bucks said, "You must travel about very carefully. There are hunters out and about everywhere." And wouldn't you know it, as soon as he emerged in the deerskin and began to chase after the does, he was shot with an arrow by a man from his very own tribe.

But the Deer-Woman isn't exclusive to the United States. Rather, her kind has been seen all over South America, Spain, and Portugal. The Scots even have a goat-legged enchantress known as the Baobhan Sith, who uses her vampire-like fangs to drain blood from men, women, children, and even livestock if the pickings are slim.

INUIT IJIRAQ AND THE QALUPALIK

Hell is not full of fire and heat and burning. Hell is a cold place, dripping with ice and falling snow. It is a place where you will never feel the reassuring warmth of fire on your bones, but you will be surrounded by the watery grave of your irredeemable sin. You will never feel warmth ever again. Shivering and trembling for eternity. Snot constantly running down your nose and fluid always in your lungs. Deep in the Arctic, where the Ijiraq and the Qalupalik call home, is as close to Hell for a human as one is likely to get while still alive. The Devil isn't about heat or warmth. His kind is icy, cold, and unforgiving.

—From the diary of Tenebris, The Boogeyman

THE INUIT'S LEGENDS of the Ijiraq and the Qalupalik are some that are perfectly in line with your classic boogeyman tales, chock-full of repulsive creatures, a pouch big enough to conceal a child, bloody death, and parental warnings of dire circumstances. But these tales revolve around the frozen oceans and glacier formations that are all around the Arctic region. As if polar bears and wolves weren't bad enough, the Eskimos now had to deal with these detestable water-dwelling carnivores whose hunting methods were akin to the black widow spider: waiting for the bait to fall into their trap.

Looking vaguely humanoid, the Qualupalik and the Ijiraq have blue-greenish skin, long hair, and talon-like fingernails. Hiding in the water near open parts of the glacier, they are quick to reach up from the water and snatch their prey below the water, enslaving them in their underwater kingdoms. In this case, I suppose, it was a fate worse than death: forever alive, forever cold, forever enslaved, until they become an Ijiraq themselves. While the Deer-Woman was at least easy on the eyes, Qualupalik and Ijiraq tend to resemble members of a Swedish death metal group in full corpse make-up.

But unlike the Qualupalik, the Ijiraq can shape-shift into any creature it desires. Again, it was Tenebris playing with the whole "improvisation" element of his job, allowing the creature born of his imagination to adapt to any surrounding he chose. Their home is the place between the living and the dead, that shadow realm where souls are trapped and become an eternal source of energy for the Ijiraq to feed upon. The Ijiraq homeland is said to be cursed, giving off a disorienting feeling of confusion and disarray whenever humans come to close to it. Those who believe they have encountered the Ijiraq and its homeland find themselves wandering aimlessly in all directions, unable to find their way. Even experienced Inuit hunters who know the areas backward and forward have experienced this feeling of uber-vertigo, losing hours of time and becoming lost in places they've been to thousands of times before.

But tribal elders are wary of calling the Ijiraq "evil," believing them to be merely misunderstood, for they are really just messengers from a higher power, and the feelings of disorientation come from the territory, not the Ijiraq. But it does little to explain why the Ijiraq and the Qalupalik play tricks on humans, like stealing their children and taking them to the middle of nowhere so they can die of exposure, or frightening hunters so badly that they drop dead of a heart attack right there on the frozen tundra.

I suppose it probably does get boring out there sometimes. A monster *does* need a hobby, after all.

NAVAJO SKIN WALKERS

BEFORE I GO any further, I do want to reiterate that the dark dealings of the one do not reflect the teachings of the many. Native people sought a higher, more defined connection to the Earth and all of its inhabitants, with special attention being placed upon the idea of an all-powerful god. In most cases, he was referred to generically as The Great Spirit. But just as there is light in the world, so too is there darkness. Christians go to it, as do Jews, Muslims, and Hindus.

The idea of the spirit animal in Indian culture is to provide that link between humans, nature, and animals, to cultivate a mutual respect for all life no matter how insignificant it appears to be. I have always seen my spirit animal to be the American buffalo or bison; their magnificent size betrays their gentle inner beauty and nobility. But if you were to truly rile up a buffalo, you had better have swift legs that will carry you pretty far pretty fast.

This notion of the spirit animal no doubt inspired the legend of the Navajo Skin Walker, a magical human with the ability to transform into any animal at will. It is definitely related to the werewolf legends of Europe (and the wolf-like beasts are the most popular of the Skin Walker legends). But the difference is that the Skin Walker can choose the animal it wishes to transform into, becoming a bird, wolf, bear, or even a snake. Whatever form suits it best for the situation it is in, it will become that animal.

But the power of a Skin Walker is definitely not a divinely given one. Rather, the Skin Walker title is handed to priests or witches who commit the act of murder, incest, or necrophilia. Any of these acts destroy the humanity within and allow the priest or witch to fully immerse themselves in true witchery. Their initiation into this Witchery is complete when a Navajo "Black Mass" is performed to curse instead of heal, and while not every witch is a Skin Walker, it should be noted that every Skin Walker is a very well-practiced witch.

Stories have persisted over the years of Skin Walkers breaking into homes to get at the people inside. They'll bang on the roof or walls outside, tap or knock on windows. Imagine the horror of waking from a deep sleep and seeing the strange eyes of an animal-like creature peering in your window, trying to get inside, wishing only to rip you to shreds. But be careful when you do spot a potential Skin Walker; the beast can project itself into you and place you under its power with only a glance. Robbing you of your energy and life force from within, the Skin Walker could leave you completely immobilized if he doesn't take your life first. Skin Walkers are also seen on lonely roads trying like hell to cause a devastating car accident, but because of their speed and incredible agility, they will always elude capture if their attempts to make you crash fail and you decide to give chase.

Another weapon at their disposal is the so-called "Corpse-Dust," a poisonous powder made from the bones of dead twin children and blown into the faces of its victims. The victim is besieged by horrifying convulsions, followed by agonizing death. A similar act is used by sorcerers and voodoo priests in Haiti and other Caribbean islands to create "zombies," though true death is not a result. While the victim lies in a very still, death-like coma, researchers believe the "Corpse-Dust" of Voodoo priests causes a certain type of neurological impairment that makes the victim more susceptible to suggestion.

Stories abound about the Skin Walkers, with eyewitnesses claiming to have seen deer jumping over fences on two legs like a man would, and of old women who run off at incredibly fast speeds when confronted—or perhaps the tale of the two fighting dogs who saw they were being watched and ran off on their back legs as a human would.

One of my own favorite stories concerns a Navajo family that was driving home one night and witnessed a six-foot-tall coyote running across the road on its back legs. The family saw it so clearly that they still remember, to this day, the white stripe running down its tail. Its appearance was marked by an ear-splitting scream that was heard over the rumble of the car's engine and radio.

SASQUATCH

PERHAPS THE MOST famous Boogeyman in all of folklore isn't really a Boogeyman at all, yet his legend has become infamous in both American and Native folklore as a terrifying beast. Now, the lore of Bigfoot-related creatures in North America is a hearty, hefty load and one fraught with varying and/or opposing ideas. Every specialist in the field of Cryptozoology has their theories. Because of this, I will only focus on what Tenebris has told me personally, the folklore of the tribes and the resulting sightings prior to 1950 that marked the beginning of the so-called Bigfoot phenomenon in American pop culture. That being said, let's get started and see where Sasquatch really came from according to the person who, rather obnoxiously at times, claimed to know him best.

> Sasquatch was not one of my creations, but a good and close friend. He was one of the few apes who had never fully evolved into that of a human, like many of his ancestors had before. Because of this,

he felt compelled to hide himself and his people away from the more populous lands. I convinced Sasquatch to come to America via that lovely Siberian land bridge. Before, he'd made a pretty nice life for himself in the snowy mountains and forests of Russia, China, Tibet. But he was growing tired of the cold and sought warmer climates. He never believed me at first, but I persuaded him that once he crossed into Alaska and headed South, he would find lush forests, warmer climates, and exotic game the likes of which he'd never seen before. My intent was two-fold: help out an old friend, as well as plant the seeds of fear into a culture that had never seen anything like him. In time, his entire tribe came over and they adapted nicely into a culture that was begging for their legend. Now his descendants are seen all over the United States. It genuinely is a pleasure to see an immigrant, who came here with nothing, truly make something of himself in this land of opportunity.

— Tenebris, The Boogeyman, (Interview 11/15/2015)

Known as Bigfoot, Yeti, the Abominable Snowman, the Skunk Ape, Devil Monkey, Yowie, and literally hundreds of other names, Sasquatch is the most well-known folktale in the history of mankind, with historical roots covering the entire Earth. But the legend of Bigfoot seemed to exist long before there was a name for him and details of his appearance and disposition tended to be different from one tribe to another. Stories of primitive "Wild Men" stalking the woods first began in the forests of Washington State and Oregon, circulating through the indigenous Lummi tribe, who are thought to have "Sasq'ets." British Columbia professor J. W. Burns would eventually take that name and anglicize it as "Sasquatch," a name that became a collective term for all bipedal, fur-covered, hominid-type creatures.

Universally described as being close to nine feet tall with brownish-black fur covering its body, the Sasquatch is thought to weigh anywhere between 280 and 1,000 pounds. Sporting an omnivore diet, our Sasquatch will feast on nuts, vegetation, and wild fruits, as well as wild game like rabbits, fish, and other small animals.

But truly, the Sasquatch's reputation as a "boogeyman" doesn't apply to the legend in this day and age. His habitat is fairly remote and removed from most of the civilized world. However, when the forest was literally at the door of settlers and Indian tribes, his appearance was fearsome and unwelcome, especially during the winters when food sources would be in short supply. Like a bear or raccoon, Sasquatch would overcome his fear of humans and seek out food wherever he could find it, and it would usually be in a log cabin, smokehouse, or Indian village.

Sasquatch encounters were terrifying simply because those who experienced it had no idea what they were actually seeing. Stories prior to 1900 are the best evidence for Sasquatch's existence, for those unfortunate prospectors and trappers were able to describe, in vivid detail, a fearsome Ape-Man that, up until that point, only the Indians had seen.

In 1900, gold and quartz prospectors Harry Colp and his friends, John, Charlie, and Fred, headed out to a remote portion of Alaska near Thomas Bay to pan for gold and mine quartz near a body of water known to the local Indians as Half-Moon Lake. Each of them began panning at different sections of the lake, separated by a few miles of each other. While the other three were off on their own, Charlie would later describe how it was that he ended up passed out in a canoe floating down Thomas Bay near Sukhoi Island.

Charlie had found a mineral-rich slab of rock overlooking the lake and he started chipping away, hoping to harvest enough quartz to make the trip worthwhile. After several hours, he grew frustrated from the lack of decent quartz and gold in what he thought might be a generous lode. But his frustration peeled away when he caught sight of three Sasquatch running toward him through the forest. Frightened, Charlie turned and tried to run, but the sheer speed of these creatures was mind-boggling. He would later describe their rancid smell, the thickness of their coarse fur, and the heat of their breath upon his neck. The claws on their hands reached out for Charlie, and their ear-splitting roars pulled at his fear even more, pushing him farther and faster. When he finally reached his canoe at the lake side, he rowed away quickly before passing out. He awoke to find himself drifting aimlessly near Sukhoi Island. The Sasquatch were no where in sight.

Such stories are common among the men of the mountain, but most people, including Charlie's friends, wrote them off as the delusions of men who were either drunk, lonely, or both. Face-to-face sightings of Sasquatch are rare; most tales tell of how the Sasquatch will stalk their campsites, throwing rocks at them from the dark or destroying their tents and looting their provisions while the campers are away on a hunt or nature walk, leaving huge footprints, mysterious fur samples, and plenty of broken branches in their wake. Even today, the stories of Sasquatch sightings continue to accrue and really show little sign of slowing down. But while many see the Sasquatch/Bigfoot legend to be merely a campfire story gone incredibly viral, there are those scholars and experts in the field who believe that Sasquatch is still very real.

"The fact is no one knows what these creatures are or knows where they come from," says Bigfoot expert Chris McDaniel, a cryptozoologist from Columbus, Indiana. "Some people don't believe that there is such a creature. If this was the case, then how would one explain thousands of eyewitnesses worldwide, of all walks of life, who have claimed to have seen these creatures? Many eyewitnesses have stated, 'I didn't believe in such a thing until I seen it with my own eyes.'"

Bigfoot authority, author, and cryptozoologist Joedy Cook agrees, remarking in an interview with *Supernatural Magazine*, "There is more circumstantial evidence of the existence of Bigfoot than there are used against convicted people in prison. Bigfoot is in every culture around the world! What is the conflict with science classifying Bigfoot as something other than a cryptid?"

Certainly, recent television shows and movies have revived the public interest in Sasquatch; most who seek him do so gently, knowing he is camera-shy and that he can be absolutely terrifying if his comfort zone is breached. But while he invokes fear and fascination for many, he is so much more to the Indian tribes who place his visage at the top of their totem poles to be worshiped like gods. They were looked upon as god-like protectors of the forest who deserved respect and adoration. The Indians know that Sasquatch lives and understand that he is a very real beast in a world undeserving of such nobility.

TWO-FACE
("SHARP ELBOWS")

SHE WAS A vain woman, a woman who longed to be one with the gods. This woman, who sought out salvation by becoming one of them, cursed herself with her own selfish needs when she attempted to seduce the great god of the Sun. In one of the most popular legends of the Sioux nation, the tale of Two-Face begins with this woman who disgraced herself and the gods by seeking carnal lust among them. To punish her, the Sun God transformed her into one of the most horrific monsters in native folklore.

She wasn't the first, nor would she be the last.

The legend of Two-Face goes back to the earliest known inhabitants of the Plains, namely the Sioux, Cheyenne, and Omaha tribes. In what can only be described as "ogre-like," Two-Face is usually depicted as a massive, humanoid person with, literally, two faces: one in the front, and one in the back. Rows of horns and protruding bones are said to be circling her head like a morbid crown. Her purpose is clear: to torture, kill, and eat her victims, which are usually women and children. While the front face does the most eating, it's the back face that one needs to avoid. Those who lock eyes with the back face will be automatically paralyzed with fear before Two-Face turns and makes you its next meal. Two-Face's main weapons are her sharp, bone-like elbows, which look like large, craggy swords ripping through the arms. Using her sharp-elbows, it maims, mutilates, and disfigures its prey.

Most tales paint Two-Face as a monstrous, evil creature, even in those tales where she is shown in the most positive light, meaning that there really is no redeeming quality about Two-Face that can be found. A very good illustration of just how malicious Two-Face really is can be found in the Omaha tribe's story of The Twins. An Omaha woman, pregnant with twin sons, was left at home alone when her husband went out. Like he did every time he left, he warned her: "If any strange person comes here while I am out, just don't look at him. You could be in danger." One day, an old man came to their home. The woman sat with her back to him, not looking at him, observing her husband's warning. The old man came back the next day and, still, she did not look at him. On the third day he returned to the lodge again, but the woman still would not look at him. But on the fourth day, when the old man came back, the woman couldn't stand it any more and she turned to look at him. A Two-Face stared back at her, and she fell over dead the moment their eyes locked. The Two-Face dismembered her corpse and ate it. The Two Face took one of her unborn babies and tossed it in the woods, but he didn't notice the other baby. The Two-Face skulked out of the lodge-house and back to where it came from. When the husband returned home, he knew exactly what had happened. Before he had time to even grieve his wife, he noticed that their baby was still alive, writhing helplessly in the remains of its mother. He never realized there had been two babies, so he took this as a sign that the babe was left alive for a reason.

Meanwhile, out in the woods, the other twin baby had been taken in and cared for by a mouse, which fed him and looked after him. The baby grew up wild in the forest, while his brother grew up to be a hunter like his father. Years later, the two boys met again and somehow knew that they were brothers. Forever bonded now, they would go on to become revered heroes of the tribe with many heroic stories to their credit.

THE FLYING HEADS

The Great God hath sent us signs in the sky. We have heard uncommon noise in the heavens and have seen heads fall down upon the earth.
—Tahayadoris, a Mohawk shaman, October 25, 1689

THE IROQUOIS, OR Mohawk in the Iroquois Confederacy, are one of my favorite tribes. They are fierce, outspoken warriors who were some of the first to witness the arrival of European immigrants. They were also the first citizens of New York, which goes to show you that New Yorkers have always been thoroughly bad ass. They were major players in the French and Indian Wars, and their chiefs are among the most respected in history. So honored and respected were the Iroquois that, when it came to their boogeymen, Tenebris made certain that they were represented well by one of the most terrifying phantasms in any branch of folklore around the world.

The Flying Heads are just that: disembodied heads with massive wings sprouting from each side, allowing them the ability to fly. The Heads have speed and agility thanks to the wings, and they use them to every advantage they can. Merciless hunters, it was nothing for the Flying Heads to run down and destroy their fleeing prey in an instant. Legends tell of the Flying Heads destroying homes and shelters, haunting the darkest parts of the forests, and bringing pestilence and plague to cursed villages. When they managed to be still long enough to land upon the earth, they still were able to stand taller than any tribesman. To top it all off, they had long, thick, lustrous hair that covered their eyes when they were at rest. When they were flying, however, the hair came away from their faces and revealed devilish, enraged eyes. To see one of them chasing you would probably be the most terrifying thing you have ever seen.

Flying Heads are usually the result of murder, but it was also widely believed that it was the punishment bestowed upon cannibals by the gods. There were also those who believed the Flying Heads to be minions of the gods, sent to do their dirty work upon people who had offended them.

But the true origin of the Flying Heads lies in a 500-year-old fable that has changed very little over the course of time. It tells the story of a village of Iroquois who somehow managed to really cheese off their gods. In turn, the gods drove away all the wild game during a particularly harsh winter. The lakes and streams failed to yield any fish. Hostile tribes dotted the lands around them, which made migrating closer to the moose and deer herds a dangerous option. The few supplies they had managed to squirrel away were gone within weeks. Famine came quickly as whole families began to die.

The older people of the village, who had been cursed by the gods, believed that if they endured the curse, the scourge against them would eventually pass. But the younger people desperately wanted to move on, take the gamble, and try to survive. Of course, the will of the Elders won out, enraging the young ones. They killed the Elders of the tribe and offered their bodies up to the Master of Life (otherwise known as *the*

God.) Decapitating the bodies and burning them, the youth of the tribe tossed the heads into a lake. But instead of being appeased by the offering, it only managed to tick the gods off even more. The heads of the Elders rose up out of the lake, spread their new wings, and continued to terrorize the tribal youths until each one of them was dead. Their impulsive, contemptible acts bred a newer, deadlier curse that is as feared as much today as it was then.

CHAPTER SEVEN

CREEPERS IN RED SUITS AND HOLLOWED-OUT TURNIPS

HOLIDAY HORRORS AND HI-JINKS

Halloween is a given, really. It's my night to shine as children, and some festive adults, all compete to be me. I adore Halloween. Christmas, on the other hand . . . well, you must admit there is a darkness on the edge of that town as well. Christmas is as ripe for terror and moral punishment as any other day, perhaps even more so. No other day of the year has the fear of being naughty been so important.

—Tenebris, The Boogeyman, (Interview 11/17/2015)

CHRISTMAS MONSTERS

THE NIGHTMARE BEFORE *Christmas* was the perfect film. It fed the fun parts of both Christmas and Halloween to children and adults alike, mirroring the magic and fun of both holidays equally well. When you ask people about their favorite holidays, no doubt both Christmas and Halloween come up the most. And why not? The terror of Halloween night, the glorious anticipation of Christmas . . . it all feeds the same giddy thrill in all of us. So it comes as little surprise that Tenebris himself has his gnarled little toes dipping into those same waters as well, spreading his tentacles of fear around jack o' lanterns and Christmas trees.

Tenebris loved the film too, though he hardly resembles the "Oogie Boogie" and it is infinitely more unsettling whenever he breaks out into song, though I promised him I wouldn't write about what is now known as "The Flock of Seagulls Karaoke Incident."

The boogeyman's interest in Christmas and Halloween monsters began very early on in the traditions, almost from the very beginning. For the first time in a millennium, children lay awake in their beds, not in fear of the boogeyman, but in anticipation of Santa's arrival. It could be said that he saw the potential immediately and put into action a series of monsters that would inhabit the fringes of the holidays while Santa skulked about quiet homes in the warm glow of lamps lit especially for him.

"Honestly, a grown man stalking about a house in the dead of night, leaving presents for children seems a bit twisted to me," Tenebris once said. "Why not leave them on the doorstep? Why the need to break in and prance about eating cookies and filling up old socks with year-old candy canes sneezed on by demented little people in green tights? It just smacks of some kind of weird, delusional, psychotic behavior. But *I'm* the weirdo."

KRAMPUS

BY NOW, MOST people know of the Krampus, most likely from the 2015 film of the same name. But few realize that the legend of the Krampus is literally just as old as the legend of Santa Claus. Tales of the horned, cloven-hoofed demon of Christmas drifted out of Austria, Germany, and Italy at first, as opposed to the Dutch region that first told of tales of Saint Nicholas, the man who would become Santa Claus.

The story of Krampus is one shrouded in mystery, but his birth from the mind of Tenebris is as crystal clear as the wine glass he was sipping from when he told me how Krampus came into being. Folklorists and legend-keepers seem to enjoy linking him to witchcraft, covens, and other forms of pagan worship. But his true origin, while laced with some Norse and Pagan aspects, has more to do with the Christian faith than with any kind of Pagan belief.

It all began years and years and years ago in the realm of the Norsemen, the true cradle of both historic and modern-day folklore. The Norse goddess Hel presided over the lands named after her, Hell. Within that realm, she held sway over the cursed dead and the damned. She was a daughter of Loki, a Norse god who specialized in trickery and deception until he was forcefully imprisoned by Odin, king of the gods, until the end of time itself.

Krampus was born to Hel as a fearful demon. With the lower body of a massive goat and the upper body of a man with generously sized horns rooting from his beast-like head, Krampus was quite the sight to behold. Standing well over eight feet tall with an energetic personality to match, he was no doubt quite a handful to rein in. Imagine an eight-foot-tall demon child, high on too much chocolate and given way too much time on his hands, and you start to get a picture of what life with Krampus was all about in the Underworld.

Early twentieth-century Austrian painting of the Krampus at work. (*Artist unknown.*)

"I really aimed to test Hel's patience with him," Tenebris would say. "Finally, she tossed him out and said, 'Come back when you've burnt off some of that energy!'"

Set loose on the world, Krampus stalked through the wintry nights, constantly mistaken for Yeti and Windigo, but trudged on nonetheless until he met a young Dutchman in a red and white snow suit piloting a team of reindeer through what would now be known as Austria. Initially hoping to terrorize him and send his soul to his mother, the unflappable man in the red suit instead lamented his job.

"He told Krampus, 'I love the children, and I love bringing toys to the ones who are good. But to the ones who have been naughty and incorrigible all year long . . . *Hurumph!* Even coal is too good for them!'" Tenebris explained. "It was then that Krampus hit upon the idea that would cement his name in the world."

That idea was to team up with the man named Nicholas, and while Nicholas would reward the goodness of children, it would be Krampus who would reward the naughty ones. Known as the "Dark companion of Saint Nicholas," Krampus would visit naughty children on the night of December 5, widely known as KrampusNacht, or "Krampus Night." Visiting the homes of the naughty, Krampus would steal into the bedrooms of children, a sack flung over his shoulder and a long-pointed switch in his hand. Swatting at them with the switch, Krampus would stuff the children into his sack (or in some regions, his large oaken bucket) and take them to his mother, Hel, where they would be burned and punished for their misdeeds.

"That seems a bit harsh," I interjected. "Especially so close to Christmas. That would ruin everyone's pudding."

But Tenebris just shrugged. "They should never have picked up the matches if they didn't want to get burned by the fire."

Truth be told, Krampus is not an evil being. Known as Santa's Shadow, he merely set about to do the work for which Santa Claus had no stomach. Punishing the naughty and the wicked was a harsh job, but it was one Krampus was born to do, and it was ultimately Santa Claus who made the call to employ his horned friend as his enforcer. Basically, Krampus did a sweep-and-clear of naughty children well before Christmas Eve, leaving the way open for Santa to spread his goodwill to good children on Christmas.

As the mythology of Krampus grew and spanned the regions of Europe, he began to take on the more demonic look of the Christian Devil, complete with horns, hooves, and a long, forked tongue. Artists of the time even began to paint him in this way, complete with chains on his hands that had been broken, as if he had just recently broken away from his prison in Hell, but Krampus purists insist the chains symbolize his enslavement to Santa.

"Rubbish," Tenebris claimed. "He was no slave to anyone. The chains were terrifying and the sounds they made in the middle of a dark and wintry night were absolutely bone-chilling. He knew what he was doing. Those chains were the best, and cheapest, prop ever. Worked like a charm."

The story of the Krampus was spread about in another attempt to get children to behave and for the most part it worked very well. Legend of the Krampus found life on distant shores, and he even made it to the United States in the early 1800s, most likely brought to the States by Austrian and German immigrants. His visage marked postcards and lithographs and frightened new generations of children into behaving. But the children of America would not be frightened for long; becoming jaded and fearless in their brazen attempts to score good loot, the Krampus legend seemed to die out as the love for Santa Claus and his gifts increased. In time, Santa reluctantly took on both roles; candy and gifts for the good and small lumps of coal for the naughty.

"I see all of those so-called 'Black Friday crowds' and I do believe that it's time Krampus returned to Christmas, don't you think? Too much emphasis on acquiring things and hurting others and all that nonsense. It's not the Christmas spirit, is it? No, I think I shall have to revive Krampus and show those who truly are naughtier than naughty a little thing about respect and caring for each other over the care of a television or crock pot."

"Why do you care?" I ask. "You spend your life terrorizing people already. I mean, it doesn't make sense if you want to punish others for doing the same thing."

For a moment, Tenebris glared. He looked as if he wanted to breath fire, but his face softened a bit and he said, "I'm not human. I have never been human. I have no idea what it means to be 'human.' It is not one of my skill sets, as it were, nor should it be. I differ from other creatures in the world, but does that make me want to destroy them, or take what they have for my own, or ruin the dreams to which they aspire? Not in the least. I inspire growth as much as I inspire fear. You humans have every reason and every opportunity to be good to each other, and sometimes, you take that chance. But more often than not, you act out of self-serving reasons. You don't hate each other, but that is not your greatest sin. Your worst sin is remaining completely indifferent to the suffering of others, even when it is you who causes it." Tenebris paused, calming himself a bit before saying, "One day, people will understand. One day."

I left it at that.

GRÝLA, THE CHRISTMAS OGRESS

ICELAND IS ONE of those places that seems steeped in magic and mystery, hidden both in plain sight and under layers of ice, snow, and volcanic rock. Like other Scandinavian countries, Iceland also has their share of villains and monsters. One of the more terrifying ones is the Grýla, an enormous ogress who lives in the caves dotting the snow-capped mountains surrounding the many different villages below.

According to legend, she lives in the caves with her third husband and their thirteen monstrous sons near the Dimmuborgir Lava Fields. Dimmuborgir is the place where Christian Norsemen believe Satan landed when he was cast from Heaven by God. Superstitious Icelander's believe the Dimmuborgir to be the entrance to Hell's catacombs, and it seems a perfect place for a child-eating ogress and her family to live. It is also where Tenebris claims to have come into existence, rising up from the fresh lava flow before it cooled and hardened.

From the darkness of her cave, she stirs a pot of broth that will soon become a stew as it heats over a fire of downed fir trees. The Grýla was said to resemble Krampus slightly, not only bearing twisted horns and cloven hooves, but also a baker's dozen of serpentine-like tails and a huge nose riddled with warts. Hanging from each of the tails was a large bag that could hold up to twenty children each. Long, curved fingernails

The Dimmuborgir Lava Fields of Iceland, birthplace of The Boogeyman and home to Grylla, the Christmas Ogress, and her fairly messed-up family. (*Photo by Ronile, used courtesy of the Creative Commons License via Pixabay.*)

adorn each massive hand and frost-blue eyes stare out from the back of her head.

Grýla was serious about her child-catching, a fact not lost on the frightened children of Iceland. From the villages below, she'll hear the sounds of Christmas and she'll know it's time, for once the carols begin, so will her search for the naughty and the main ingredient for her yearly stew. Leaving her cave, Grýla the Ogress climbs down the mountain and into the villages, seeking out the ones who smell of mischief and disobedience. Lured to them by her insatiable appetite and her uncanny ability to detect wayward children, she will devour some as they sleep in their beds, and steal the others to add to her stew pot.

According to old tales, Grýla was married three times, first to Gustur and then to Boli. But Grýla would outlive both men. How the husbands died is a mystery, but it could be hypothesized that Grýla most likely ate them for being insolent. Her third husband, meanwhile, left her well enough alone to do as she pleased, possibly because he remembered what happened to her previous husbands. One cannot blame him for taking a backseat to his ravenous wife. In any case, these two human men gave Grýla her thirteen sons, though it was thought that, being so obviously fertile, Grýla most likely had more.

In the more popular legends, the 13 Yule Lads were named after their specialties of deviousness. They were:

Stekkjastaur (Sheepfold-stick)
Giljagaur (Gulley-oaf)
Stúfur (Shorty)
Thvörusleikir (Spoon-licker)
Pottasleikir (Pot-licker)
Askasleikir (Bowl-licker)

Hurðaskellir (Door-slammer)
Skyrgámur (Curd-glutton)
Bjúgnakrækir (Sausage-pilferer)
Gluggagægir (Peeping-Tom)
Gáttathefur (Sniffer)
Kjötkrókur (Meat-hook)
Kertasníkir (Candle-beggar)

In the thirteen days prior to Christmas, each son would descend upon the village and dole out his unique brand of mischief until the last night when Grýla herself would go into the village, scoop up the naughty, and take them back to her cave to devour.

Icelandic parents got so good at weaving twisted tales of the Grýla and terrifying their children with this ogress that a public decree was written up in 1746 prohibiting the act of traumatizing kids with the Grýla, forcing mom and dad to get more creative if they wanted little Billy to behave. Despite the decree, stories of the Grýla still get passed around to this day, but now, her sons leave gifts in empty shoes and opt to wear red and white snow suits like a certain bearded, jolly fellow. But the Grýla is still described as a monstrous creature intent on filling her belly with the rich meat of children who refuse to obey their parents.

Sometimes, you just can't keep a good Boogey down, and why try?

THE WHIP FATHER

HIS STORY IS one of the most bizarre tales of Christmas boogeymen, ripe with blood, horror, and cruel punishment, and yet it is such an obscure tale that very few deviations on the original legend actually exist. It is one of the purest folktales in all folklore because of this, and that makes it my new favorite tale.

Originating from France, the tale of The WhipFather (or *Le Père Fouettard*) begins with an innkeeper in a remote, isolated region who has fallen on hard times. His family has abandoned him, business was at an all-time low, and he didn't have enough money or food to survive. With the onset of winter and the coming holidays, provisions would be even harder to get. The innkeeper, known as Serge Babineaux, was a desperate man, and when desperate men are featured in folktales, their exploits are anything but heroic.

On Christmas Eve one year, the inn was completely empty, as it usually was, and Serge sat alone at his desk, lamenting his station in life. All he had to look forward to was the sale of pork that was sitting in a barrel of brine in the corner. While it would bring in *some* money, it wouldn't be enough by far to survive the winter. A grand idea came into his head when three boys walked in. Garbed in expensive hunting clothes and carrying equally pricey rifles, the three youths demanded a room. They'd been hunting in the mountains all day and were willing to "slum it" in Serge's mountaintop inn. Not only was Serge extremely happy to have lodgers again, he was

Santa and "The Whip Father." (*Artist unknown.*)

even more elated to see the boys' large coin purses, filled to the brim with gold and silver pieces.

Serge immediately set upon the boys, cutting their throats. As their blood crept across the wooden floor and their money jingled in his pants pockets, Serge began to cut them into pieces and dumped them into the barrel of brine, increasing the weight and thereby increasing his take when he sold the meat.

Lo and behold, Serge's perfect plan was interrupted by none other than Santa Claus himself, who caught him in the midst of dismembering the first boy. But Santa does two amazing things next, the first of which borders on being Christ-like. He brings the three boys back to life and sends them on their way, presumably with a candy cane in each hand, before setting his sights on the murderous Serge once more. But rather than take him to the authorities, Santa Claus takes the law into his own jolly hands and condemns the murderer to an eternity of service as his new helper, the Whip Father. He would serve at Santa's side and punish the naughty children on his list, doling out both lumps of coal and vicious beatings to the errant children of France.

"There's clearly no better punishment for a child-killer than to take him on a holiday joyride of bondage and sadism," *Cracked* writer Jonathan Wojcik once wrote. Between Krampus and The Whipfather, "Clearly a step or two needs to be added to [Santa's] pre-screening process."

The Whip Father is garbed in dark clothing and carries a thick chain around his neck, the end of which leads to Santa's scrupulous mittened paw. His hair is long and gray, as is his beard, and the hair is scraggly and unkempt. A sinister glower is forever etched into his face, and he carries with him a handful of birch tree switches, all ranging in size and thickness.

Today, the Whip Father is quite the sensation, having both a Facebook and a Twitter account and is rising just as quickly as Krampus among the jaded youth of today. His presence signals the emergence of the darker fringes of Christmas into the limelight, and whether that's a good thing or not is up for debate, but it certainly makes the holiday a lot more interesting.

> It is a good thing the name "Whip Father" stuck when it did. It
> certainly is a lot more terrifying than Father Spanker or Count
> Switch-a-Lot, which was Santa's first choice. He may have been a
> stellar humanitarian, but he suffered dreadfully at marketing. It was
> a good thing I was there to advise him.
>
> —From the diary of Tenebris, The Boogeyman

THE NISSER

NOT MANY PEOPLE are aware of it, but Tenebris is an incredibly talented creature that can whip up a beautiful crepe and a plush cup of hot cocoa, but undoubtedly, his greatest talent lies in crafting complex legends and folktales that are richly detailed and exceptionally well-rounded. We have discussed his work in the Netherlands and Scandinavia at length already, but in the spirit of Christmas, I'd like to showcase one of his more unusual and fantastic creations, the mysterious Nisser.

Though not directly related to Santa Claus, Nisser is known as a gift-giver and a saint of the winter solstice. He is usually seen to be around three feet tall with a long, white beard wearing a gnome-like cap. The Nisser is thought to be the spirit of a farmer who cleared portions of the forest to build his farm and brought the spirit of Christmas to the nearby villages. After his death, the farmer was buried on the farm. That Christmas marked the first arrival of a very odd, small man who bore a striking resemblance to the farmer. Looking very garden gnome-like, Nisser took to living in the barns and houses of farmsteads across the Swedish countryside (where he was called Tomten in the late 1800s), acting as the guardian of the family, protecting the livestock and crops from wild animals and disease. Treat them well and Nisser would reward you with protection and aid in chores around the farm.

When offended, Nisser would become a short-tempered little creature capable of mischief on an epic Mogwai-type scale, including stealing things, playing tricks on the family, killing livestock, and destroying the crops he once swore to protect. He's particularly incensed by lazy and abusive farmers, those farmers who think nothing of beating their horses and oxen, or using their living spaces as a toilet. Such mistreatment of animals will result in a sound thrashing from Nisser, and nothing is worse than getting your ass handed to you by a three-foot-tall gnome who happens to possess immense strength. To avoid insulting the Nisser, leave a bowl of porridge with butter for him on your doorstep, a surefire way to thank him for the work he's done for you.

But you have to *leave* the porridge for him. Norwegian tales of Nisser have been told where he will even engage women in combat, usually after they eat his porridge. One unfortunate maid decided unwisely to pilfer the Nisser's breakfast and paid for it by being beaten within an inch of her life by the creature, known playfully as "dancing with the Nisser." Charming.

What makes the Nisser so complex is that he tests your will to be a good person by using his ability to shape-shift. He may take on the appearance of a homeless man in need of help, or maybe a wounded animal in need of medicine. Whatever form he chooses, it is one that will ultimately reveal more about you than it will about the Nisser. Before the onset of Christianity, the Nisser was viewed as almost Christ-like to a degree, performing miracles, rewarding faith, and punishing the wicked and corrupt.

But after Christianity spread into the region, legends of the Nisser were imbued with demonic attributes and much darker motives. His bite became poisonous, treated only by Christian healing ceremonies. Farmers who continued to view the Nisser as a guardian of the farmsteads were seen as heretics worshipping false gods or demons. In fact, the belief in the Nisser led many feuding neighbors to falsely accuse each other of witchcraft and devil worship, which, in turn, led the way for torturous inquisitions and mass hangings of suspected witches. In time, the literature began to change to reflect the Nisser's now notorious reputation; translator's began to decipher stories from the Brothers Grimm and Hans Christian Andersen, substituting the word "goblin" for the word "Nisser."

Eventually, poets and writers began to try to reverse the bad image of the Nisser, most notably with the 1881 poem "The Tomten," by Swedish writer Viktor Rydberg. In the poem, the Nisser (now referred to by his Swedish name, Tomten) is alone and awake on Christmas Eve. As he moves forlornly through the house and barn he holds watch over, the Tomten/Nisser ponders not just the meaning of life, but also the meaning of *his* life. By the end of the poem, it would seem that Rydberg is alternately mourning and celebrating this once magical legend of Swedish lore. I find the poem to be tragic and a moving piece, evoking a sense of loss wrapped up in a glittering package of promise. It has since become a holiday staple for many grade schools around the world and is still enjoying immense popularity in both Finland and Sweden.

HALLOWEEN BEASTIES

WITH HALLOWEEN AND its accompanying beasties, we have a holiday full of many different things for many different people; it's one of the reasons why people revere it so much, but to appreciate the origins of Tenebris's Halloween Horrors, we must go back to where it all began, the ancient Irish festival of Samhain (pronounced "Sawween").

Founded by Celtic Druids, the festival of Samhain took place on October 31 as a way to observe the ending of summer, the harvesting of crops, and casting out of the old and moving into the new. More importantly, it was the one time of the year the Druids believed that the souls of the dead walked freely among the living, returning to their old homes and farms to visit with the families they left behind. But human spirits weren't the only things roaming about on Samhain, soon to be known as All Hallows Eve. Evil spirits, banshees, shape-shifters, and faeries would come and go frequently, tricking and tormenting the living. To ward off these evil apparitions, the Druids would light huge bonfires and wear ugly masks and disguises to befuddle them into thinking they were one of them. Other means of spooking the spooks included making large amounts of noise to agitate them so much that the spirits would move on willingly.

The spirits who *were* welcome, however, received offerings of food left outside the doors of their old family homes. Apples were a favorite treat in that all apples had to be harvested before the feast of Samhain began, or the evil faeries known as the Puca would spit on them as they hung in the trees, leaving them bitter and inedible.

STINGY JACK AND HIS LANTERN

One of the oldest Halloween traditions revolves around the jack o' lantern, certainly an indispensable tradition for All Hallows Eve, but one that began with the chilling story of a devious, manipulative scumbag known as Stingy Jack.

Jack was well known about the villages of Ireland as a famous drunk, fighter, and quite a silver-tongued devil. His reputation as a malicious shyster even got the attention of the Devil himself, who confronted Jack on a cobblestone path in the middle of the night following one of Jack's bouts with the bottle. The Devil had come to earth to find out if the rumors of Jack's evil were true or not, and when Jack saw Satan standing before him, he figured his time was up, that his chips had been cashed in, and this was his fate.

Somehow, Jack convinced the Devil to let him have a last drink before following Satan back into Hell. Surprisingly, the Devil allowed it, even taking him to the pub himself and plying Jack with enough liquor to float a battleship. When he'd drunk his fill, Jack brazenly asked Satan to pay the tab; he convinced the Devil to transform himself into a silver coin to pay the bartender. When Satan did just this, Jack whipped the coin up into his hand and stuck it in his pocket . . . right next to a silver crucifix, which prevented Satan from turning back. Now wielding the upper hand, Stingy Jack forced the Devil to agree to let him go for at least another ten years. Begrudgingly, the Devil agreed, transformed back into his old grouchy self, and returned to Hell.

Ten years passed and Stingy Jack once again found himself face to face with the Devil, who obviously had been chomping at the bit to get at this fellow. But again, the Devil fell prey to Jack's devious nature. When Jack claimed hunger, the Devil climbed up a tree to pluck an apple from the branches for him. But once in the tree, Jack surrounded the base of the tree with silver crucifixes, trapping the Devil once more into giving Jack what he wanted. This time, Jack demanded that he not ever be taken to Hell at all. Again, the Devil agreed, and Jack removed the crucifixes.

Eventually, the drinking and dangerous lifestyle took its toll on Jack and he died. As Jack went to enter Heaven, he was stopped by St. Peter, who told him that, because of his sinful lifestyle, deceitful practices, and excessive drinking, he would not be allowed into Heaven. He was sent, instead, to the Gates of Hell but found the way blocked by Satan, who would not renege on his pact with Stingy Jack and allow him entry. But the Devil wasn't all bad about it. He gave Stingy Jack a glowing ember of coal inside a hollowed out turnip, the epitome of a warning that Stingy Jack was a denizen of Hell. From then until the end of time, Stingy Jack would roam the place between the living and the dead, carrying only the glowing turnip to light his way. Over time, the turnip would become a pumpkin, and Jack's ghoulish lantern, now referred to as a jack o' lantern.

SPRING-HEELED JACK

In nineteenth-century London, there were often reports of ghosts and phantoms plaguing the dark streets, black masses and wispy spirits of the dead crawling across cobblestone and dancing in the black air of tunnels, alleys, and other narrow passages. Some say the sightings were a by-product of the burgeoning spiritualist movement, a sort of mass panic of having sat in on too many spooky séances. Others believed that the new awareness of spirits simply made them more visible, that they'd been there all along.

But one entity that stood out above all others was the notorious phantom nicknamed "Spring-heeled Jack." He was so famous that he became the subject of numerous books of the time, horribly written "penny dreadfuls" that emphasized his outlandish looks and uncanny ability to make extraordinary jumps from building to building, which is, of course, how he got his name. He also became quite an icon of Halloween festivities given his macabre appearance and terrifying method of operating. Prank-loving boys and even grown men took to dressing up as this thing for parties. Kind of like the Victorian-era version of us dressing up like Canadian serial killer Paul Bernardo or the "Nightstalker" Richard Ramirez for Halloween parties. Yes, it was *that* classy.

First appearing in newspapers in the fall of 1837, sightings of the bizarre Spring-heeled Jack soon spread all over Britain, Ireland, and Scotland. With his clawed hands, silver helmet, eyes of burning red, and flowing black cloak, he was indeed a sight to see in Victorian-era England (though today he would be a popular attraction in Piccadilly Circus or Times Square in New York.) Tall and stringy with a drifter's build, he was still able to maintain the appearance of a civilized man, and a few witnesses even claimed he spoke to them in intelligible, almost polished English. At the same time, other witnesses claimed he would breathe blue and white flames. It is not hard to see how he influenced modern-day superheroes and villains like Batman and The Crimson Ghost.

Prior to the appearance of Spring-heeled Jack, however, was the emergence of what was called the Hammersmith Ghost in 1803, a demonic entity notorious for attacking Hammersmith residents as they walked the streets at night. Many of the same attributes, such as its ability to leap incredible distances and its outlandish appearance, would later be used to describe Spring-heeled Jack to a tee. Appearing only three times, in 1803, 1804, and 1824, the Hammersmith Ghost legend quickly gave way to the very prolific and active story of Spring-heeled Jack in 1837 when he allegedly attacked a servant girl on her way back to work after visiting with her parents. Snatching her from the mouth of an alleyway, Spring-heeled Jack held her still with his strong hands, which she described as "cold and clammy as those of a corpse." He tore at her clothing, kissing and touching her flesh with animalistic passion. The attack abated when she screamed bloody murder, sending Spring-heeled Jack off into the night. A search party was launched to find her attacker, but no one matching his description would ever be found.

Attacks on unsuspecting women continued to occur at an alarmingly predictable rate, but police were completely baffled. Newspapers and writers from all walks of life and culture aimed their pens at Jack, using his villainous, and completely lecherous, actions to sell more papers, magazines, and books. Embellishing the initial attacks and imbuing Jack with supernatural gifts turned his story into a modern-day legend.

Spring-heeled Jack continued his crimes against women and fashion for over a year before the first break in the case. The police had arrested a man named Thomas Millbank, who was caught wearing white overalls and a great, flowing cape. Tall and wiry, he fit the description of Spring-heeled Jack; in addition, he was heard boasting in the Morgan's Arms pub that he was, in fact, Spring-heeled Jack. He escaped conviction only because one of the witnesses insisted that her attacker had breathed fire upon her, a talent Millbank denied having. So, of course, they had to let him go.

Sightings of Spring-heeled Jack continued, but ultimately declined in the late 1840s. His legend enjoyed a resurgence in the 1870s and again in the very early 1900s, with the last sighting of him being reported in 1904 on William Henry Street in Liverpool. While most concede that Spring-heeled Jack was one or more people with a very macabre sense of humor, I had my doubts. In my conspiracy-theory-addled mind, I could not put to rest the fact that Spring-heeled Jack sightings ended in the 1870s and didn't start again until 1904. Was Spring-heeled Jack also the notorious Ripper of 1888? I asked Tenebris his opinion, and The Boogeyman smirked.

"Let's just say this. I'm not saying Spring-heeled Jack was Jack the Ripper, but tell me: Have *you* ever seen them together in the same room?"

CHAPTER EIGHT

A NEW LEVEL OF NIGHTMARE

THE RISE OF THE AMERICAN MONSTER

My work was done, essentially, when America was born. Take that statement however you like.
—Tenebris, The Boogeyman, (Final interview 11/18/2015)

WHILE TENEBRIS AIDED the Native Americans with his power to raise monsters, he did so too with the immigrating Europeans. But his work was short in that many of the fears they brought with them had been born, bred, and spread about in the Old World long before thoughts of travel had even crossed their minds. But America, truly, is a melting pot of cultures, monsters included. Most all of the minions of Tenebris in the United States have their origins in England, Ireland, Scandinavia, and other parts of Europe, and while their roots are firmly planted abroad, the fruit that is yielded is clearly American. With the passage of time and the rough edges of the average American, the boogeyman became meaner, nastier, and far less forgiving than he had before.

RAWHEAD AND BLOODY BONES

Rawhead and Bloody Bones
Steals naughty children from their homes,
Takes them to his dirty den,
And they are never seen again.

SO BEGINS THE nursery rhyme of Rawhead and Bloody Bones, one of the most terrifying tales of monsters to ever come out of Great Britain. Born in a pool of blood curdling in Celtic soil, the branches and leaves of Rawhead and Bloody Bones spread across the pond and into the wilds of America, where the story quickly became known as terrifyingly real.

Rawhead got his start in a 1548 pamphlet called "Wyll of The Deuyll" (Will of The Devil) written by English poet George Gascoigne. Blatantly anti-Catholic, the story is basically the last will and testament of the Devil, dictated by Satan himself to his secretary in the Court of Hell, Rawhead and Bloody-Bones. Rawhead's station in Hell was confirmed in a sermon penned by an Anglican minister in the year 1566, who warned his parishioners that "Hell and the Devil" need to be taken as seriously as "Grandmother's tale of bloody bone, raw head, and Ware woulfs [werewolves]." Obviously, the minister was peeved that more attention was being paid to old wives tales and scary stories than the exploits written about in the Holy Bible.

"It backfired," Tenebris added. "Those who didn't know about him before learned *everything* about him after that sermon."

The tale of Rawhead and Bloody Bones seems, at first, startlingly simple as the villain is generally seen as a typical, ogre-type beast. But Rawhead's story is much more than that. Legend has it that he was a settler who had farmed over sacred Indian land. In exacting a horrible revenge, the Indians scalped the farmer and sacrificed him to a guardian demon. This demon took the farmer and created Rawhead, an enormous beast with constantly running wounds from his ferocious scalping and a horrifying, beast-like appearance. For all eternity, he would roam the wilds seeking shelter and would never find anything permanent or comfortable. In addition, his hungers would only be satisfied by the blood of children who had dared to look him in the eye. Rawhead would sneak into houses, barns, and cellars at night, seeking shelter underneath stairwells and in cupboards near the basement. He sits in hiding, waiting to strike at the curious children who dare to look under the stairs. Those who do, see the horrific Rawhead sitting atop a pile of bloody bones, patiently awaiting his next meal. To those brave kids who averted eye contact, they walked away with a terrifying story to pass on to their kin and friends. But to those who were unlucky enough to lock eyes with Rawhead, they became his next meal and the freshest set of bloody bones for Rawhead to recline upon.

In some legends, Rawhead and Bloody Bones are two wholly different creatures, working in tandem to generate as many sleepless nights as possible. In this case, Bloody Bones is usually seen as a headless skeleton that tends to dance alongside his beastly cohort, a sort of diabolical Bonnie to Rawhead's Clyde. Stories of Rawhead and Bloody Bones are usually told as a morality tale, such as the ghastly duo who tears the tongue from a well-known gossip monger, or rips the arms off a man seen as a belligerent pugilistic bully. More often, and more terrifying, is the tendency for Rawhead and Bloody Bones to be seen as random night stalkers who take whomever crosses their path.

As the story grew legs and traveled West, Rawhead and Bloody Bones became less of an ogre/skeleton dream team and literally became a wild razorback boar that stalked the untamed wilderness. The most famous story of this part of the legend comes from Missouri, which concerns a witch by the name of Old Betty who lived alone in the woods. Her only friend was a boar named Rawhead, who looked out for the old woman and considered her just as much a friend as she did him.

Whether it happened by accident or was malicious retaliation for a wrong committed by Old Betty, Rawhead was shot dead by a local hunter, who butchered and ate the wild hog. Enraged, Old Betty conjured the spirit of her murdered friend, transforming the once-benign hog into a beastly, enormous man wearing the skull of Rawhead as a helmet. With fiery red eyes and a blood-streaked body, Rawhead and Bloody Bones set out to murder the hunter, tearing him limb from limb before skulking off into the night. Still fueled by indomitable hatred for humans, Rawhead began stealing children and devouring them in his favorite hiding places, such as basements, the cupboards under dark stairwells, and in the sodden rooms of out-cellars. The outrageous and terrifying legend of Rawhead would eventually inspire a robust number of books and movies, most notably Edward Levy's novel, *The Beast Within*, Richard Laymon's darkly perverse and brilliant novel *The Cellar*, and the grisly *Rawhead Rex*, a direct adaptation of the British legend written by Clive Barker.

To this day, there are Rawhead aficionados who still believe in their demonic monstrosity, who still fear the night, and dread the beast who lurks in the darkest parts of the wooded hills and forests. To them, the threat is real, the beast exists, and to see its fiery eyes is to seal your own fate.

BUNNIES, GOATS, AND MOTHS . . . OH MY

Seems to me that this bit would work better in your chapter on urban legends, but that's none of my business.
— Tenebris, The Boogeyman, (Final interview 11/18/2015)

THE BUNNY MAN

FOR SOME REASON, the idea of human/animal hybrids freaks out a lot of people and its a tactic that Tenebris uses regularly to elicit a spike in someone's heart rate. While legends of Europe and Asia played with the ideas of animalistic people such as werewolves, it wasn't until America was born that the fully-formed idea of a human-like animal came to pass. Technically, the Bunny Man doesn't fit into the category very well in that he was a deranged human dressed as a rabbit, but we cannot split hares when it comes to the boogeyman.

The story of the Bunny Man is one of those rare instances where urban legend mingles nicely with a good ghost story, making it the total package in terms of its qualities as a good tale, even as the ghost story becomes a part of the legend and vice-versa. And as outlandish as it will sound, the Bunny Man's origins stem from a series of documented attacks, printed in newspapers of the time and recorded in police logs and ledgers. This isn't that uncommon, really; all urban legends have their roots planted firmly within irrefutable truths and the Bunny Man is no exception.

Tales arose of an insane man dressed like a white rabbit who escaped from an asylum near Fairfax County, Virginia, despite the fact that no such asylum ever existed. Ever. But from that jumping-off point, tales of the Bunny Man multiplied. Implicated in the tale as well was the now-infamous Bunny Man Bridge where supposedly two teenage boys and a teenage girl were found murdered, their bodies gutted and left to hang from the bridge on Colchester Road. According to legend, the Bunny Man returns every Halloween Night to kill more trespassing teenagers.

Those are the legends, extraordinarily vivid and violent accounts, yet wholly false and undocumented, that arose from the chance meeting a few people had with a disturbed young man in the woods of Fairfax County, beginning in October of 1969. While Air Force Cadet Bob Bennett and his fiancee, Dusty, thought they were dealing with a deranged whacko in the woods, they were in fact dealing exclusively with Tenebris, who had created the guise of the murderous Bunny Man after catching sight of a Ku Klux Klan rally.

> There was a fear in the Klansmen that fell prey to my intentions
> . . . they dressed in white sheets in order to look like ghosts, to rile
> up the superstitious, but to me, they just looked like giant bunny
> rabbits with an awful vocabulary and horrendous body odor. Inci-
> dentally, when I first donned the Bunny disguise, I was actually
> confused for one of those god-awful Klansmen.
>
> —From the diary of Tenebris, The Boogeyman

Bob Bennett and his fiancee, Dusty, had been visiting some relatives of his on Guinea Road in the small town of Burke. They had stopped and parked their car in a field, the engine still running as they apparently talked "about their feelings for each other." It was well past midnight and the rural area was dark and fearsome, far from the security of the city's lights. Surrounded in darkness, it is little wonder that the two soon became a little freaked out when they began to notice movements from behind the car, seen out the rear window with their alert peripheral vision.

Suddenly, the driver's side window shattered and the two looked in horror at a man clad all in white standing outside. Panicking, Bennett slammed the car into reverse and pulled away while the man in white screamed at them about their flagrant trespassing on his property. "You're on private property and I have your tag number!" he'd screamed. As the two drove away, trying to catch their breaths, they noticed a hatchet lying on the floor of the car, supported on a bed of broken glass. Bob was certain that the man was wearing a bunny suit with long bunny ears, but Dusty was adamant that they were Ku Klux Klan robes with a white hood that came to a point.

The Klansman/Bunny Man conundrum continued until all debates were silenced nearly a full year later on October 29, 1970. Construction security guard Paul Phillips approached a man standing on the porch of an unfinished home on Guinea Road. The man was wearing a gray, black, and white bunny suit and seemed to be about twenty years old, was about five-feet-eight inches, and weighed about 175 pounds. The Bunny Man began chopping at a porch post with a long-handled ax, muttering to Phillips: "All you people trespass around here. If you don't get out of here, I'm going to bust you on the head." Needless to say, Paul Phillips did just that, but police were unable to find and apprehend the disturbed young man in the bunny suit.

These last two encounters were reported to local police and printed in the local newspapers. They are the only time an encounter with the Bunny Man has actually been documented as fact, yet they are bizarre enough to spawn a whole slew of Bunny Man stories that spiderweb and fork off into many different directions.

But all roads lead back to the bridge. Bunny Man Bridge. It became Ground Zero for the Bunny Man, not out of choice, but of necessity. It was never a spot where the Bunny Man was known to frequent, but it was close enough to the actual site. Once the original Bunny Man stopped his inane bunny-suited rantings, Tenebris grew a snarling, nasty little demon with big ears that would haunt the rubes frequenting the bridge.

To say strange things have happened there is an understatement. The bridge has gone from being a favorite stop for legend trippers to becoming a mandatory stop for burgeoning paranormal investigators, leading police to install cameras on both sides of the bridge, its electronic eye searching out vandals and mischief makers. The legend of the Bunny Man is something that plagues Fairfax County, bringing more bad than good to this quiet—and private—little slice of Virginia wilderness. But is there anything to it?

The story of the Bunny Man is one of those classic fables in which a very real, very human incident becomes a monstrously elaborate legend. The Bunny Man is no longer a disgruntled man in a costume, but a vengeful, vaporous monster that is both everywhere and nowhere. That's Tenebris, and he saw you coming a long time ago.

In my own hometown, there is a haunted bridge that, if you flash your lights three times, then honk three times, you'll see the body of a young man who hanged himself dangling from the bridge. I never saw anything myself, but it was a good ploy to freak out the girls brave enough to join my friends and me. In truth, the legend of that particular bridge grew out of a story of an unfortunate boy who fell from the bridge, but survived. The basic evolution of legend works extraordinarily well when blended with the twisted imagination of a being that has devoted its life to the development of fear.

"Are you talking about me?" asks Tenebris.

I roll my eyes.

THE GOATMAN

Unlike the Bunny Man, the Goatman is all monster, resembling the Pan-like satyrs of Greek mythology, and sightings of the beast have been far more plentiful, occurring in states as varied as California, Texas, Florida, and Michigan. But the most prolific of the Goatmen is the one who lives in the caves near Bowie, Maryland.

He first appeared in the area in 1957, seen as a hairy, horned beast darting through the trees. He wasn't spotted again until 1962, when he was accused of killing a total of fourteen people, twelve of them children, a death sentence imposed on them by the Goatman for hiking too close to his cave. Those who survived testified that the Goatman hacked his victims to death with an ax, roaring and grunting as he brought the edge down again and again. Oddly, or perhaps not surprisingly, the police have no record of the incident and no stories of the Goatman's massacre ever made it to the papers.

Interestingly, the Goatman's origins are just as fantastic as his exploits. Some say he was conjured during a series of Satanic rituals, others claim he is an escaped mental patient, and a few believe that he was manufactured in a genetics laboratory by the United States military (a legend Goatman shares with the infamous Chupacabra of Mexico and Southern Texas). This particular aspect has come up more often than the others when tales of the Goatman arise, though most folklorists accede that the Goatman was centered around the Beltsville Agriculture Research Center in Beltsville, Maryland, rather than around the town of Bowie. Experimenting on himself with goat DNA, the scientist in charge wound up going mad and taking out automobiles and pedestrians in the area before disappearing into the woods.

Like the Bunny Man, Goatman also lays claim to a bridge, known as Governor's Bridge in Maryland, where he skulks about seeking victims to dismember and devour. In fact, the stories are so similar that it is more than just a little possible that the two legends are indeed the same folktale told by different people. Sightings of the Bunny Man in the 1970s seemed to coincide with sightings of the Goatman around the same time frame at Governor's Bridge in Maryland. Both legends hearken back to the old English tales of trolls and ogres living in or under bridges and having their ways with gullible travelers, signs that the tales weren't based on any real truths, but rather adapted to fit the climate and landscape of America. In short: same story, different place with a much more visceral ending.

> The Goatman was never that good. He was just *ba-a-a-a-a-ð*. Don't be sheepish, boy. For goat's sake, that was a good joke. No, I kid. I kid.
> —Tenebris, The Boogeyman, (Final interview, 11/18/2015)

THE MOTHMAN

In contrast, the Mothman of Point Pleasant, West Virginia, is said to be an almost benevolent creature, interested in the survival of mankind rather than focusing on being the cause of its undoing. He was first spotted on November 12, 1966, by five gravediggers in a cemetery in Clendenin, West Virginia. As the men worked that night, they all reported being "buzzed" by a human-like, winged creature with red eyes. A few nights later, Roger and Linda Scarberry of Point Pleasant reported seeing a large white creature with glowing red eyes. With a wingspan of nearly ten feet, it was not hard to be freaked out when the two realized it was flying close behind them as they drove home. Over the next year or so, the Mothman continued to appear to different people from all walks of life, including police officers, construction workers, and regular working folks. Some believed that the Mothman wasn't anything other a giant sandhill crane, and the majority of citizens almost preferred the supernatural legend.

The sightings seemed to come to a head on December 15, 1967, when the Silver Bridge collapsed, causing the death of forty-six people. No other sightings of Mothman were reported after this incredible disaster, leading many to believe that the two incidents were connected. As ludicrous as it sounds, the release of John A. Keel's 1975 book, *The Mothman Prophecies*, wherein the investigative journalist tried hard to connect the Silver Bridge disaster with the appearance of the Mothman, alluded to an alien/UFO influence in said appearances. In addition to sightings of Mothman, eyewitnesses claimed to see odd flashing lights in the sky at night as well as mysterious Men In Black coming and going on a regular basis. Something truly odd was at work in Point Pleasant and way too many reliable people were seeing so many different things.

"This planet is haunted by us," wrote Keel in *The Mothman Prophecies*. "The other occupants just evade boredom by filling our skies and seas with monsters."

While there is no disputing the fact that the Silver Bridge suffered a fatal crack in a suspension I-beam that led to its collapse, Keel theorized that Mothman had attempted to warn the citizens of Point Pleasant that something would happen by repeatedly appearing and using his alien influence to cause unexplained electrical disturbances and phone line interruptions. The film version of Keel's book, also called *The Mothman Prophecies*, was released in 2002 and attempted to focus more on the supernatural aspect of Mothman's erratic behavior and bizarre appearances, which many see as prophecy.

"Whatever the creature may have been, it seems clear that Mothman was no hoax," writes author and researcher Troy Taylor. "There were simply too many credible witnesses who saw 'something.' It was suggested at the time that the creature may have been a sand-hill crane, which while they are not native to the area, could have migrated south from Canada. That was one explanation anyway, although it was one that was rejected by Mothman witnesses, who stated that what they saw looked nothing like a crane."

It wasn't a Mothman. It was Birdman Larry. He just got lost on his way back to Florida. Most people thought he was an enormous moth, but he was actually a Thunderbird. Vastly different, and if you call him Mothman to his face, he will let you know how much you rubbed him the wrong way.
— Tenebris, The Boogeyman, (Final interview 11/18/2015)

The Thunderbird was a legendary a pre-Columbian Native American creature that resembled an eagle with what has been described as a twenty-foot wingspan. Arguably one of the oldest monsters in history at just over 10,000 years old, it is a legend that has appeared in nearly every single tribe in North America and was responsible for destroying, not only the giant horned snakes that threatened the earliest peoples of America, but also the elephantine lizards that once threatened to overrun the land. They are seen as messengers of the Sun Gods, sacred beings that live in cloud-covered mountain ranges in the sky. So sacred is the Thunderbird that its image has appeared on native homes, totem poles, archaic petroglyphs, blankets, and clothing of the native people, who bear its image in hopes that it may bring them protection.

And, apparently, one of them is named Larry.

THE JERSEY DEVIL

The deepest, darkest forests always have the best monsters. It's really almost impossible to count the number of legends, folktales, monsters, madmen, beasts, and creatures that found their places haunting the dense sea of trees and foliage around the world. The only locations that rival the forest in terms of shrouded secrecy are the barely explored lakes and oceans of the earth, but we won't be discussing Nessie or Ogopogo here. Rather, we turn our attention to the absolutely most dreaded monster in American history.

In realistic terms, the Jersey Devil shouldn't exist, yet there are thousands of eyewitnesses who have testified to its authenticity, and millions of stories that ignite our imagination. Some say that it was created out of a need to disgrace rival politicians and almanac writers of the time, notably Quaker-born writer Daniel Leeds, whose named was linked to the Devil mythos from the very beginning. In any case, its legend casts a dark pall over the seemingly tranquil and beautiful appearance of the Pine Barrens of New Jersey. Close to the Eastern coastline, the Pine Barrens is packed with exotic plants, trees, and bogs and swamplands. Because of its unusually sandy soil, it is virtually impossible to farm. The only things that will grow there are the multitudes of pygmy pitch pines, several breeds of orchids, a number of different carnivorous plants, and a very healthy wellspring of wild animals. Even before the Jersey Devil came into the world, it was a place known as "Popuessing" by the Lenape Indian tribes, which means "place of the dragon." Later, Swedish explorers would add their own exclamation point on the area by naming it "Drake Kill" (the Swedish words for "dragon" and "river").

The New Jersey Pine Barrens, c. 1901. *(Photo courtesy of the Library of Congress.)*

But it wasn't until 1735 that the tale of the Jersey Devil changed the Pine Barrens area forever when the Leeds family unwittingly invited the Devil into their lives and the lives of all others who would venture into the mystic woods.

In a place now known as Leeds Point in Atlantic County, Japhet Leeds and his wife, Deborah, had carved out a decent life for themselves and their twelve children. Japhet was most likely a logging man, working nearby in the Pine Barrens as his wife raised their children. But by the time she became pregnant with her thirteenth child, Deborah had had enough. Tired of being pregnant for most of her life and most likely at the point where her babies could probably just walk out of her womb, she cried out in disgust, "Let this one be the Devil!"

True to form, as it happens in all legends, when the Devil is called, the Devil arrives.

On a dark and stormy night, Deborah Leeds went into labor with her thirteenth child. As thunder rumbled, lightning cracked, and rain pounded the small wooden house, her midwife delivered what appeared to be a normal, healthy baby boy. But as it opened its eyes and uttered its first cry, the baby changed. His feet became hooves. Bat wings sprouted from his back, along with a forked tail that curled and wound around the midwife's trembling arms. His eyes turned blood red, and what came from the baby's mouth was more of a pained howl for blood than it was a cry of innocence as he greeted the world. Murdering the midwife, the Devil Baby flew around the room, screaming and growling as it flew up the chimney and into the stormy night. Circling the villages and surrounding towns, it was finally spotted flying into the maze-like Pine Barrens.

For years, the beast haunted the Pine Barrens, leaving the corpses of deer, rabbits, and other small animals in its devilish wake. Those who hunted him came home to tell their families of hearing horrific roars from unknown beasts. There were even a lucky few who claimed to have seen the Jersey Devil, flying in the night sky, recognizable from its imposing silhouette against the moon. The legend grew locally, becoming a fearsome tale told around Atlantic County fires and dinner tables. There were several who dismissed it as drivel, but to the superstitious families of the area, it was an absolutely real threat. The most famous sighting would be recorded in 1909, but it wasn't until December of 1925, 190 years after its birth, that the Jersey Devil made worldwide news.

Artist's interpretation of the Jersey Devil based on eyewitness accounts. Published in the *Philadelphia Post* in 1909, this illustration is still the most widely accepted version of the famed beast. (*Artist unknown.*)

A farmer in Greenwich Township named William Hymer claimed to have killed the Jersey Devil following a brutal fight with the creature that ended when he fired his rifle on the beast. The "Devil" had been caught by Hymer stealing and eating chickens out of his hen house. Amid claims that over 100 different people could not identify the dead creature, no photograph of the body was ever taken, nor was any autopsy or examination of the body ever performed. But with all the earmarks of a clever hoax, sightings of the Jersey Devil continued, with some sightings coming in from as far west as Pennsylvania, and as far east as Salem, Massachusetts.

But most of the stories that come out about the Jersey Devil are the products of wild imaginations and an itch for blatant hoaxing, going back as far as 1909 when Norman Jeffries (no relation) used the Jersey Devil to keep his ailing museum from closing. Jeffries was a notorious publicist for Philadelphia's Arch Street Museum, and faced with the loss of his job, he declared that the Jersey Devil had, indeed, been captured. Along with his best friend and co-conspirator Jacob Hope, Jeffries purchased a kangaroo from a traveling circus, attached fake claws to its front paws and glued equally fake bat-wings to its back. Put on display at the museum, the "Jersey Devil" attracted thousands and kept the struggling museum open. Surprisingly, most people needed to be told it was a hoax, which Jeffries did twenty years later.

While much of the hubbub surrounding the Jersey Devil leads to obvious skeptical conclusions, there are still those who venture into the

Pine Barrens on a regular basis, intent on finding that which hasn't been found in more than 250 years. Still, people traveling down the Garden State Parkway or the Atlantic City Expressway have reported sightings of something odd or unknown flying through the air, or darting across the busy thoroughfares, stories that continue to fuel the speculation that the creature *does* exist in one form or another. The Philadelphia Zoo posted a $1,000,000 bounty on the Jersey Devil in 1960, a bounty that still stands today (though nowadays it is mostly for show than the real offer it was back in 1960).

But according to Tenebris, the truth behind the Jersey Devil is far simpler and perhaps a lot darker than most are willing to believe.

Darker than the Devil, you say?

"Well, that's a matter of opinion," he told me. "None can be darker then Old Scratch, but I do try."

According to Tenebris, after he'd arrived in the New World, he found himself enjoying the Pine Barrens and the supernatural air of it when he happened upon the Leeds family in Atlantic County and—more specifically—Deborah Leeds. "She was so beautiful," he said, his tone quiet and mournful. "She looked exhausted, but it hardly bled out her natural glow. So, so beautiful. I actually felt that push of love inside me when I looked at her. Like a ball of light in the pit of my stomach that reached out from the inside."

Entranced by her beauty and drawn in by her effervescence, Tenebris visited Deborah Leeds at night as she slept, crawling into her dreams and becoming that which she was missing in her life: the thrill of youth and vibrance she felt she'd lost long ago. In her dreams, she and Tenebris walked through faerie woods and climbed mountain peaks, seeking out sun and laughter and life. Her marriage to Daniel Leeds had been blessed by God and Tenebris could not break that seal, no matter how much he wanted to, and so he was indeed shocked when he learned that Deborah had become pregnant with their child during one of their dalliances in a dream.

"All that happened after was true," Tenebris finished, lowering his head. The pain of such an old memory was obviously still there after all these years and it made my heart ache for him. "The child—*my* child—was born a shape-shifter, which is why no one has been able to find him, thankfully, and after all these years, no one ever will. He can become the Devil you seek, the rabbit hiding in the brush, or even that illustrious sandhill crane that is revered for its grace and beauty and mistaken for a giant flying moth. But at least he's safe."

IN SEARCH OF FROGMEN

On the outskirts of Lafayette, Indiana, my current hometown, lies a small town named Dayton, which is incidentally where I grew up and spent the best years of my life. But in all my years of running around the back roads, fishing at the Wildcat Creek, and walking the train tracks with my best friends I never knew that, right in my back yard, there was a legendary creature lurking in the dark. It was the first Boogeyman I ever knew, and Tenebris, like he was for every nightmare, was the primary force behind its inception.

A mile or so outside of Dayton near the highway is a thoroughfare called Richardville Road. It empties out onto Wyandotte Road and ends at the top of the hill. Today, the area is known for its lush cornfields and quiet living. But in the mid 1790s, it was mostly unusable swampland full of frogs and snakes. The mushy bogs would be filled in with soil and rock from land near the Dayton Cemetery sometime after the events of this story.

Before, the land was used for a small Indian village named Richardville, named after Jean-Baptiste Richardville, a Miami Indian Chief who would go on to become the richest Native American landowner in the United States. He was the son of a French military officer named Joseph Drouet de Richardville, and a woman named Tacumwah, who was sister to the presiding Miami Indian chief. Known as Peshawa (which means "wild cat"), Chief Richardville took land offered to him by the United States government in the St. Mary's peace treaty of 1818. Richardville used the land to raise his family and owned several trading posts across the area, which only served to increase his already immense wealth. But in 1829, the Richardvilles sold off their land to Samuel Mc-George, a farmer and horse breeder who specialized in raising race horses.

This is where it starts to get interesting.

Most of Richardville was incredibly fertile and grew amazing rows of corn and

The former site of the Richardville Swamp, now filled in and used to plant corn. No sign of the beast was ever uncovered during the immense work it took to fill in the old swamp. (*Photo by author.*)

soybeans. But then there was the Richardville Swamp, an ugly scar of a bog in the middle of all that fertile ground. According to legend, the Richardvilles avoided the area, not even using it to trap fish or turtles. The swamp was a constant source of frustration for the McGeorges. They always seemed to be short when it came time to harvest whatever crops they could get to germinate and pay their bills. Sales of the race horses slowed down considerably. If they could farm the swamp, they'd have enough to get by on. Samuel McGeorge tried to devise a way to fill up the swamp and be able to farm it properly.

In the summer of 1830, as he was walking the property one night, Samuel heard a loud splash in the darkness. Lifting his lantern high, he saw the shiny, thick-skinned body of an enormous creature walking on its muscular hind legs. Its face was almost frog-like and it had two long arms that swung at its sides with thick muscles packed onto them. Standing nearly seven feet tall and dripping with the black water of Richardville Swamp, the beast struck an imposing profile in the darkness.

Samuel tried to run, but fell as he tripped over a tree root. The lantern shattered beside him, covering him in fiery oil. Panic seized him as he tried to put out the fire and avoid the beast walking toward him. But the amphibious beast stepped forward and used the flat palms of its gigantic hands to swat the fire out. Confused, Samuel McGeorge looked to the beast and began to stammer out a scream that never came.

"Quiet," the beast told him. "I've heard of your quandary, and I know what you have planned for the swamp. This is my home and I don't want to lose it. But I have a plan for you. One that would benefit us both."

Dumbstruck, Samuel McGeorge couldn't move nor could he speak. But his ears worked fine and he listened as the beast continued.

"Bring travelers here, leave them for me. A few a month is all I need. I've survived on frogs and fish and snakes for so long, but I pine for human flesh. Bring me victims and you may keep their wealth for yourself. That way, you will not go into the winter in debt and I will not lose my sanctuary. Do you agree?"

"What if I don't?"

The beast looked toward the McGeorge's stately home on the hill overlooking the swamp; he admired the fiery glow coming through the windows from the fireplace inside. "Then I will destroy you, your family, and all that you hold dear. I took a gamble and allowed you to see me, all because I wanted to help both of us. But I cannot afford to risk my life living here if you and I do not see eye to eye."

Samuel McGeorge chose to strike a bargain with the beast. Raven-tressed and beautiful, Darcy McGeorge was the love of his life and he had promised her father that he would always take care of her. To him, this included financial security as well as physical security.

So, every month, Samuel McGeorge delivered a new victim to his ward in the swamp, served up to the beast alive and kicking. And when the beast was finished, Samuel McGeorge pocketed wads of cash. But like all schemes of a homicidal nature, Samuel's plot was uncovered by children who watched the beast devour an unfortunate corn broom salesman before disappearing back into the swamp.

Samuel McGeorge got news that a mob was coming for him and he promptly fled the area with his wife and child, never to be seen again. Some say he settled into a cabin in the woods near Platteville, Wisconsin, and others claim they had seen the fugitive near Sioux Falls. Still others say that he opened a pub and eatery in Sheboygan, Wisconsin, called Gilman's. (Tuesdays are Polka Nights, with the area's best prime rib and cuttlefish casserole.)

New owners took over the property and filled in the swamp. No one ever found the swamp monster the children had talked about, even after an extensive search of the area. Fishermen even dragged the deeper areas of the swamp but found no trace of the monster. In time, the soil settled into the swamp, corn was planted and harvested, and Richardville the town was dissolved, becoming part of rural Lafayette. Along with the dissolution of Richardville's status as a township, so too was the legend of the Richardville Swamp Monster, who is now barely a footnote in Tippecanoe County history. Or so says my father, who first told me this story, and Tenebris, who backed up his claims when I pressed the issue further with him.

As for the Swamp Monster himself? Tenebris claims he moved from the swamp when the first rumblings of a posse were felt and re-settled himself at what is now known as The Big Fish Campground a few miles away. There, he lives on the mud veins of catfish and the occasional pack of uncooked hot dogs and marshmallows stolen from unwary campers. Once the creature migrated south, Tenebris lost contact with him.

Incidentally, a similar creature would be spotted near the banks of the Ohio River on August 21, 1955. A mother named Darwin Johnson was swimming with her children and some friends when she felt something grab her leg and pull her under the water. She struggled and fought whatever it was that had grabbed her, and could later only describe the hand as being green with claw-tipped fingers and hairy knuckles. But as soon as she was able to shake the hand loose, it grabbed her again. Finally, Mrs. Johnson lunged for a nearby inner-tube and the beast let go, fleeing the scene.

Back on shore, it was discovered that she suffered numerous cuts and bruises to her leg. She told a fantastic story of a green-clawed monster, an outlandish tale that would have been easily dismissed if it wasn't for the green-colored bruise of a handprint where the creature had grabbed her. For several days afterward, the handprint remained until it finally faded away.

Was it the Richardville Swamp Monster?

The story caught national headlines, and supposedly the women were even interviewed by the notorious Men In Black about the incident, and no one else ever reported being attacked by such a beast. Because it occurred at the height of UFO-mania, the press and most who passed the tale around believed that the creature that had accosted Mrs. John-son was a being from outer space, but deeper research into the legends of the area point to the possibility of it being one of the mythical Loveland Frogmen or perhaps a cousin to the infamous Thetis Lake Monster of Canada, two fairly well-known tales in cryptozoological circles.

The Loveland Frogmen, based out of Clermont County, Ohio, are described perfectly in their name. The creatures resemble human-sized frogs walking on their hind legs, much like the Richardville Swamp Monster and the Green-Clawed Monster. But where the stories diverge is that, unlike the Richardville and Ohio River monsters, these Loveland Frogmen have been spotted numerous times since the 1950s, with sight-ings diminishing to zero by 1972. Businessmen, farmers, and even police officers have claimed to see small packs of these aquatic creatures roam-ing about near the Ohio River and the marshy swamps around the river banks. But whereas the Green-Clawed Monster has been actively hostile toward humans, the Loveland Frogmen have never shown any sign of aggression at all.

The Thetis Lake Monster, unlike the Frogmen, seem to be more hu-manoid in appearance, looking much like a deranged missing link between man and fish, almost as if they were once fish, began their evolution into humans, but then stopped short all of a sudden.

Calling Colwood, British Columbia home, the creature is said to reside in the still waters of Thetis Lake, appearing every so often to the horror and/or delight of those lucky enough to be passing by. Described as nearly five feet tall and weighing close to 120 pounds, the Thetis Lake Monster wears a skin of tight silver scales. Its mouth is filled with dag-ger-like teeth and an array of six spikes protrude from the back of its scaly head. Complete with black, bulbous eyes and webbed hands and feet, the Thetis Lake Monster is said to bear more than a passing resem-blance to Hollywood's *Creature from the Black Lagoon*.

While most believe it to be a wild tale and—in at least one instance, a hoax—the legend continues to hold water with the Native American people of the area, who, for generations, reported an overwhelming number of face-to-face encounters with the carnivorous water monsters.

I just wondered what a carp mixed with a frog would look like, and *blammo*! The Richardville Swamp Monster was born. Same thing happened when I wondered what a frog would look like walking around like a human. Mind you, this was *years* before Kermit the Frog answered that question for *everybody*. It happens that way sometimes. I'm not proud of it, but sometimes it creates a fabulous accident that works extremely well. This one was kind of in the middle.

—Tenebris, The Boogeyman, (Final interview, 11/18/2015)

CHAPTER NINE

REINVENTING THE GAME

THE URBAN BOOGEYMAN

There comes a time when all the past must dissipate like fog. Monsters lose their magic, creepy creatures forget their true power of fear . . . it is a grim inevitability that even the grandest monster must adapt to the changing way of the world. Old fears harden and scab over, it cannot be avoided. When that happens, you exchange the rock for the sledgehammer, and you go back to work.

—From the diary of Tenebris, The Boogeyman

A S THE MID-TWENTIETH century unfurled, humans found more realistic terrors awaiting them. From the threat of nuclear destruction to the imminent crumbling of society as a whole, humans were faced with horrors that were far more intense and realistic than that of a deranged witch in the woods, or a bloodthirsty werewolf stalking dense countrysides that no one seemed to traverse anymore.

"Jaded" would be a good word to use. "Hardened" perhaps a better one. The sickly hands of time had hurried their pace, and Tenebris foresaw the shifting tides of fear better than anyone, adopting a new strategy in his quest for fear. It was a revolutionary idea, actually, one in which Tenebris would capitalize on new fears and spread them about like a virus as he used to in the old days. In doing so, Tenebris orchestrated the birth of the urban legend, tales of monsters and madmen that would spiral in and out of people's lives, making them change their daily habits, and bringing fear past the relative safety of their front door. Monsters weren't scary anymore; Abbott and Costello—as well as The Three

Stooges and Bugs Bunny—had made certain of that. Humanity was scarier anyway, and the paranoia a strange person instilled in another was far more palpable a fright than anything Hollywood could dream up. Obviously, a true monster could be evaded or repelled, but what if that monster looked just like you?

This new tactic of terror would change the way the boogeyman was perceived and would ultimately lead Tenebris to become something he never envisioned for himself.

He would have to become human.

The idea behind the classic urban legend was fairly simple as it generally consisted of the same parts classic folktales had always had: take a well-known setting, place an innocent victim into that location, import a major morality conundrum, then slam a monstrous trauma upon them. The final step was getting the story to circulate without help from Tenebris. Back in the good old days, it could take years for a scary story to make it across one continent. But in the age of telephones, newspapers, televisions, and movie theaters, word of mouth would not only increase the paranoia in everyone who heard the tale, but multiplied the chances of it spreading across the nation in a matter of days. Each instance was a one-shot deal for the boogeyman, so each element had to be perfectly staged, choreographed, and executed with elegance and precision. It was a brilliant, though highly experimental, plan that ended up working flawlessly. Today, urban legends have replaced the rustic, old-fashioned folktale with a more contemporary setting and a grislier sensibility.

Among his best works is the classic tale of the Hook Man, one of the first of his experiments. It began one night, in August 1954, at a small cove near Wolf Lake in the mountains of Colorado. Most nights, the cove was busy with plenty of traffic, but on this night, it was eerily calm, quiet, and secluded. For Bill Johnson and Marjorie Flemming, it was a nice chance for the two seventeen year olds to be alone. As the two teenagers kissed and made-out while the radio played softly, the music was interrupted by a news anchor, desperately warning those in the vicinity of Wolf Lake that an escaped mental patient had recently been spotted in the area. Described as tall, lanky, and having a hook for a right hand, the patient had been incarcerated following a series of murders he'd committed a few years prior on Lover's Lane near Wolf Creek.

All of a sudden, the quiet and solitude became pregnant with paranoia and apprehension. After much deliberation, the two teens opted to leave rather quickly, backing out and speeding away. When Bill Johnson got out of the car at Marjorie's home and went to open her door, he sucked in breath, and his blood ran cold.

Hanging from the door handle was a large, bloody hook, looking as if it had been ripped off someone's arm.

Though not very scary today, in 1954, it was a verifiable scream. By the end of the year, most kids in the United States would swear that the incident happened in their town to someone they knew. The experiment was a success, and Tenebris followed this streamlined path to harvesting fear in a grandiose and conquering manner. Some of his contemporaries, such as the Grim Reaper (who is *very* vocal in his opinions and enjoys cigars) would say he became lazy and bloated on the fears of moral-minded teenagers, while others (like the almost always drunk Easter Rabbit) congratulated him on perfecting a sort-of "assembly line" of fear.

Most people would hardly be frightened of the story if they knew that Tenebris was accompanied on this charter mission into a new universe of terror by an unusually chatty Sasquatch, who'd found Tenebris by accident while searching for a suitable place to sleep for the night.

> He just kept saying, "I don't get it . . . I don't get it . . . You're The Boogeyman, but you're playing an escaped mental patient? I don't get it." Had the hairy baboon been there when the boy saw the hook hanging from the door handle, he probably would have let out a long "Ohhhhh . . . I get it." He never was very swift, but who needs to be when you can bench-press a Buick and you have a twelve-foot stride? Ladies loved him, obviously."
>
> —Tenebris, The Boogeyman, (Final interview, 11/18/2015)

Whatever the case may be, Tenebris took the ball and ran with it, creating highly plausible, harrowing scenarios that became famous for their brutality and sheer horror. Whether it was lacing a woman's beehive hairdo with black widow babies, hanging a dead man above a frightened girl's car, or repeatedly placing horrific phone calls to the babysitter downstairs, Tenebris succeeded wonderfully.

But teenagers thought that, once they'd grown a little and gone off to college that the terrors would stop, that scary stories were kid's stuff. No longer would there be anything to be afraid of in the night.

Again, it was an August night in 1969 that reality gave them the wake-up call they never wanted to get.

On August 9, 1969, cult leader and perennial con man Charles Manson instructed his followers to go to a house on Cielo Drive in Beverly Hills, California, and murder everyone there. The next night, he instructed them to do the same at a house on Waverly Drive in Los Feliz. In all, seven people would be brutally stabbed, bludgeoned, and shot to death by crazed intruders intent on fulfilling the wishes of their leader.

The grisly savagery and brazen attitude of the once peace-loving hippies awoke a new kind of terror that wasn't born in a mental hospital or prison. Now, the monsters under the bed were their own children, stalking them with knives and guns, and it was yet another way that America's security was ripped away. The so-called "Manson Effect" had people installing double deadbolt locks on their doors, putting up security lights, and buying handguns for home defense.

It was a more personal fear inside them now, one that reeked of invasion of privacy, of not being safe in their own homes, not from the arms of monsters, but from normal people. Out of that fear, came a new brand of terror tale. One where home is not always the safest place to be . . .

> One case in particular happened in Florida in 1973. A seven-year-old girl named Emily Fischer lived with her parents and her older sister, sixteen-year-old Judith, in a large house on a quiet street in suburban Clearwater. Not having many friends, Emily relied on the friendship of her dog, a beautiful yellow Labrador named Honey, who hardly ever left her side. Even at night, when Emily got into bed, Honey was there, sleeping under the bed. Emily would always lean her hand down the side of the bed and Honey would lick her hand, letting her know she was safe and that he was there for her.
>
> One night, Emily and Judith's parents went out for the night, leaving Judith in charge. But Judith was tired of looking after her sister constantly and she made plans to meet up with her boyfriend once their parents left. Emily protested, not wanting to be left alone, but acquiesced once Judith reassured her that Honey would protect her, and that she wouldn't be gone long.
>
> Judith left as Emily took her bath. Once she was done and in her pajamas, Emily went to bed and turned off the light. Like always, she reached her hand down the side of the bed and breathed a sigh of relief when she felt Honey lick her hand.
>
> Emily woke the next morning and screamed, for written in blood on her My Pretty Pony vanity mirror was the phrase, "Humans can lick too, my sweet." They found Honey's disemboweled body in the bath tub."
>
> —From the diary of Tenebris, The Boogeyman

"Wait, you killed the dog?"

Tenebris looked to me and sighed.

I just stared at him, dumbfounded, and I laughed nervously. "That's cruel."

Tenebris smirked a bit and said, pointed to himself, and said, "I never claimed to be a nice guy."

His point was well taken, but it was still harsh.

As children grew up and moved away, they thought they were safe. They weren't. Tenebris was always behind them, following many of them off to college, a trip that managed to scare up two of his best-known legends. The following stories are taken from Tenebris's journal, word for word.

> Her named was Ashley. A cheerleader name. She even looked like one. Soft, pure, untouched by the world. And it was into the world she was going and I was watching her from the dark. Her sweat, while it smelled like honey and heather, would soon smell rancid and dirty like everyone else. It was time for her initiation.
>
> She was attending Ohio State, majoring in journalism, I believe. I was going to give her the story she always wanted.
>
> I'd set my sights upon her roommate, a pretty girl named Jenny. I hid in the shadows of her closet until the lights went out and her breathing dropped shallowly. I knew she was asleep. Outside, Ashley would be returning to the dorm room after a late night of studying at the campus library.
>
> In the dark, I crept out of the closet and produced a small knife. I began cutting her, listening to her cries as I held my hand over her mouth, feeling her tongue against the flesh of my hand as I pressed harder.
>
> The door opened. I looked and saw Ashley's silhouette from the light outside, and I watched her reach for the light switch. Then, as if she thought better of waking her friend, left it alone and slipped into her own bed. In time, she was asleep, and I finished the job on Jenny. As the room filled with the heady iron-smell of blood, I took some of it into my hands and found the vanity mirror.
>
> When Ashley woke the next morning, she found the thoroughly ravaged body of her friend; she went mad and screamed and screamed and screamed as she looked at what I had written on the mirror: "Aren't You Glad You Didn't Turn On The Light?"
>
> —From the diary of Tenebris, The Boogeyman

For the first time since I'd sat down with him, Tenebris was beginning to frighten me. Was he truly responsible for some of the grisliest, most haunting murders ever committed? And moreover, were these urban legends actually true, the brutal machinations of a creature that couldn't exist, but did? He had gone from being an innocuous, legendary creature of faerie tales, folklore, and mythology into a remorseless, dark creature of unimaginable horror?

He looked at me as if to answer, but did so with a devilish grin. "You won't ask," he said quietly.

I shook my head. No.

"Probably wise," he said with a slight shrug. "You know the answer already anyway, I'm guessing. Why beleaguer the point?"

He was The Boogeyman. This was what he did. Turning loose the Grýla or the Dullahan upon a jaded world would result in more laughter than screams. The effects of grislier theatrics, culminating in a Grand Guignol-esque psychodrama for the masses, would have the world trembling in their beds and front seats forever. As Tenebris adapted to the gorier work of frightening adults and college kids, he found that the formula of using fear against them to create more fear could work even better. In this way, he only had to do a little to reap a lot, and so, stories of the Hatchet Man were born.

The most well-known tale of the Hatchet Man deals with a university student and her roommate at Indiana University in Bloomington, Indiana. Drew, a freshman, and Joyce, a sophomore, were roommates in the same dormitory in the late fall of 1985. In the midst of starting the new year, Bloomington police had begun warning students about a serial killer who may be stalking the area. All students were advised to walk in pairs and stay in brightly lit areas if they had to go out at night.

> The two girls opted to remain at the dorms during Thanksgiving break. But life in the empty dorms got boring quickly, and they decided to check out a local pub not far from campus. It was almost 1:00 a.m. when they decided to leave. But Drew was busy flirting with a busboy, and Joyce, somewhat drunk, decided to walk home alone.
>
> As she walked through the dark night, Joyce suddenly remembered the warnings of the serial killer at large, and suddenly, she felt as if she were being watched. She swore she could hear footsteps behind her. Breaking into a run, Joyce headed for the dormitory as fast as she could, running up the stairs and into her room. After slamming the door behind her, Joyce began to feel better, and soon, she was calm enough to lie down and get ready for bed. After taking a long hot shower, Joyce crawled into bed with a book. But almost as soon as she'd pulled the covers up, the sound of eerie scratching pierced the quiet. Coming from the front door, it sounded like fingernails scratching the wooden door.

Terrified, Joyce hunched down in the bed as the scratching continued. There *had* been something following her all along, and now it was right outside her door. Finally, the scratching stopped and Joyce was able to fall asleep.

When she woke the next morning, Drew's bed was still empty. Figuring she'd find her passed out on the lobby sofa, Joyce opened the door and screamed.

Blood streaked down the walls in rivers, and great pools of drying blood had formed underneath the body of Drew as she lay on the floor outside, the fingernails on her outstretched hand were splintered and shredded from where they had scratched desperately at the door as she was being murdered.

Across the hall, a bloody ax had been lodged in the wood jamb of their neighbors door. And me? I watched from the maintenance room while she quickly lost her mind. She wouldn't stop screaming, even as they took her away in the ambulance.

—From the diary of Tenebris, The Boogeyman

The legend of a Hatchet Man or Ax Man is not that far-fetched a story, with roots going back to a very real spate of murders that occurred in 1919 in New Orleans, Louisiana. A thoroughly deranged killer, the Ax Man of New Orleans once vowed to kill anyone not playing jazz music in their homes at 12:15 a.m. on March 19, 1919. In all, he and his ax claimed seven lives in a series of twelve attacks between May 1918 and October 1919 before he went completely off the radar and disappeared.

A similar tale took place in Villisca, Iowa, in 1912, when a mysterious killer took the lives of Josiah Moore, his wife Sarah, their three children, and two other children spending the night at their house. Like the Ax Man of New Orleans, there were several suspects, but, alas, no evidence to convict. When the Ax Man murders took place six years later in New Orleans, there were thoughts that perhaps the man responsible for the brutal slayings of the Moore family had possibly made his way to New Orleans, but, again, no evidence exists linking the two criminals.

As we ponder the meaning of life as it applies to murderers and madmen, it doesn't take much to make the leap to one of mankind's greatest fears and Tenebris's ghastliest creation.

Clowns.

One of the more bizarre, terrifying, and non-murderous tales of Tenebris's exploits revolves around a clown statue, which owes more to the near-universal fear of clowns than it does to the possibilities of what said statue could do. There is something ominous, terrifying, and suspicious about a man who paints a smile onto his face, hiding dark intentions behind a colorful palette of vibrant greasepaint and brightly colored clothes. While over-sized hands, feet, and faces may be comical to some, most see these clowny traits as monstrous deformities that puts one into a state of unease right from the get go. Add to that the thoroughly anti-social behavior of clowns in the circus (they usually deliver pies, water, or confetti to the face, or execute some other wanton behavior that infringes upon another's comfort zone) and you have the makings of what they call "coulrophobia": a fear of clowns.

Most clowns are fun-loving comedians, intent on bringing smiles to small children any way they can. Before I became strongly anti-circus because of their questionable treatment of animals, I remember having some of the best laughs of my life at the expense of truly funny clowns who had taken slapstick comedy and made a near-flawless art out of being smacked in the face with a bowling pin. But the mystique, and horror, of clowns isn't all a thing of recent times. Before John Wayne Gacy became known as "The Killer Clown," the Joker became Batman's greatest rival, and before Pennywise terrified an entire generation of Stephen King fans, clowns were staples of festivals and fairs dating all the way back to the middle ages. However, for every clown who wanted to make people laugh, there were more than a few who wished nothing but harm. Rapists, murderers, highwaymen, and thieves all found sanctuary behind the greasepaint at one time, finding it easy to hide their faces behind cheery makeup or masks. In addition, being employed by a traveling circus afforded them the opportunity to rape, rob, and murder their way through an entire town before disappearing into the night and moving on to the next town with little to no detection.

While benign clowns such as Chicago's own Bozo and his sidekick Cookie, Freddy the Freeloader, Emmett Kelly, Sideshow Bob, and Howdy Doody's best friend Clarabell remind us of why we loved being kids, it was darker clowns like Pennywise, Pagliacci, Captain Spaulding, and Spawn's Violator that reminded us why we should fear them.

But the mistrust of clowns isn't just the work of Hollywood screenwriters. In reality, some fairly sick individuals have used the clown persona to mask their sickest inner perversions. While John Wayne Gacy's "Pogo the Clown" may very well be the best-known "killer clown," he wasn't the only one. Amon Paul Carlock, a former Illinois minister, used his role as "Klutzo the Clown" to collect literally thousands of pieces of child pornography videos and photographs. He was detained in San Francisco upon his return from the Philippines after graphic photographs of Mexican and Filipino boys were found on his digital camera. After a lengthy investigation into the former minister's actions, federal agents raided Carlock's home, where they found over twenty-one child pornography videos on six different DVDs. He was arrested immediately for possessing the child pornography, as well as for practicing sex tourism. He would later die after being tased by corrections officers in jail while awaiting trial. Other killer clowns include the Czechoslovakian serial killer Frederick "Zozzaby" Zozabe, whose clownish ghost haunts children to this day, and the West Palm Beach Killer Clown, who randomly shot to death a housewife before disappearing into legend. In present-day London, New York, Chicago, and Los Angeles, instances of creepy clowns appearing in the middle of the night and merely walking around, unnerving residents with their stoic, quiet demeanor, have hit print and Internet news agencies on an almost daily basis.

In the summer and fall of 2016, the prospect of killer clowns took an ominous turn when sightings of grotesque, macabre-looking clowns began to surface all over the American landscape. Most sightings placed the clowns on the edges of forest land or in the darker corners of public alleyways, either beckoning to young children or just maintaining an eerie, silent presence as the public maintained a safe distance. These men and women would dress in smeared makeup and intentionally frightening costumes as they carried baseball bats, machetes, and meat cleavers, using both the fear of clowns and the fear of the unknown to their supreme advantage. Some blamed the rap group Insane Clown Posse, while others blamed the rash of hilarious Killer Clown prank videos populating YouTube. But as the "Clown Craze" of 2016 progressed, the fear petered out, resulting in the Clowns often getting a very exhaustive beating at the hands of a fed-up public. Wisely, following the Halloween season, sightings of the horrific clowns dwindled to almost nothing and became yet another urban legend that would surely not go away, but only bide its time until the next opportunity arose.

So when the time came for Tenebris to employ a clown into one of his newest tales, I was a bit surprised that he hadn't done it before. In the folktale known simply as "The Clown Statue," a babysitter named Darla is settling into a good book in the living room after having successfully put the baby, Katelyn, to bed upstairs. But as she tries to read, she finds her solace disrupted by the presence of a thoroughly off-putting clown statue in the living room. Standing about three feet tall with a polka-dotted white jumpsuit, the clown just freaked her out.

A few hours into her book, the phone rang. It was the child's father, asking how things were going.

"Things are great, but I have to tell you. I think I'm going to have to move this clown statue of yours. It's totally freaking me out."

There was a pause. Finally, "Darla, I want you to get Katelyn and go next door. Call the police."

"Why?" she asked.

"Because we don't own a clown statue."

Darla looked at the clown statue and now realized that the clown was looking right at her. As it turns out, the clown statue was actually a former circus worker and little person who'd been fired from his job. For the past month, he'd been living undetected in the family's home, eating their food and sleeping in out of the way spaces where he wouldn't be found. He'd been sneaking through the living room when he was surprised by Darla as she walked in. Terrified, he froze, acting out the part of a clown statue until he could safely get away.

While no death is implied or shown, the tale of "The Clown Statue" is infinitely more disturbing without it for obvious reasons. The clown would eat your food in the middle of the night, watch you while you sleep, and perhaps do even more when you think you're alone in the privacy of a bathroom or bedroom.

> Paranoia and fear is so much more delicious when you're vulnerable. You're never more vulnerable than when you're alone, or naked, or indisposed. Do these people know what watches them when their guard is down?
>
> — From the diary of Tenebris, The Boogeyman

As we wind down this chapter on urban legends, we'll finish with the tragic tale of a young woman haunted by incredible demons. What happened to Elisa Lam was haunting and disturbing; it was made all the more tragic in that what happened to her wasn't a folktale. It really happened. She was the daughter of Hong Kong immigrants and a bright, happy young woman. Stopping in Los Angeles while on a tour of California, Elisa shared a communal room with two other roommates when she checked into the Cecil Hotel near Los Angeles's Skid Row on January 28, 2013. The Cecil was a rundown hotel that had once been fairly popular, but now it was more known for being one of "Night Stalker" Richard Ramirez's favorite hangouts while he conducted his reign of terror across California in the 1980s. Aside from this morbid fact, the Cecil was nothing more than a glorified flop house where overdoses and suicides became commonplace among the residents. Soon after she arrived at the hotel, Elisa began to exhibit bizarre behavior that earned her a separate room at her roommate's insistence. In the past, she'd suffered from bouts of bipolar disorder and depression, with multiple prescriptions assigned to her to treat the conditions. According to family and friends, Elisa's mental disorders had been relatively benign and under control.

Two days later, she disappeared without a trace. Video surfaced from the Cecil's security cameras showing Elisa Lam entering one of the elevators, obviously terrified and looking about wildly for someone or something that was following her. But nothing was seen on any of the video surveillance footage, and her bizarre behavior had many speculating that she was being pursued by something paranormal, pointing out the Cecil's dark history of violence and the exorbitant numbers of suicides committed there. More plausible is the theory, given that Elisa suffered bipolar disorder and depression, that she may have suffered a severe psychotic break that caused her to lose all touch with the reality she once knew. Whatever the case may be, she was still missing.

As her parents and the police searched valiantly for Elisa, residents of the Cecil Hotel began to complain about the water coming from their sinks and showers. It was oddly colored, tasted foul, and smelled terrible. An investigation led to the roof, where four 1,000-gallon water tanks provided water for the entire hotel.

Elisa Lam's lifeless and nude body was found floating in one of them on February 19, 2013. Her clothes floated idly beside her. For twenty days, she had been lying in a public water cistern supplying the hotel, including the restaurant and kitchens on the first floor. An autopsy concluded that she had died of an accidental drowning, citing her bipolar disorder as a defining factor in the cause. There was no evidence that she had been murdered, nor was there evidence to suggest that she had committed suicide. A psychotic break would have essentially made the notion of a swim in one of the water tank's seem like a good idea. But with logic missing from the equation, Elisa most likely found that once she got in, she couldn't get back out. Tired from constantly treading water and screaming for help that no one could hear, Elisa Lam most likely slipped beneath the water and drowned.

Oddly, her death very closely mirrors the plot of the 2002 Japanese horror film *Dark Water*, released eleven years prior to her death at the Cecil hotel in 2013, which is also based on a 1996 short story by Koji Suzuki, the internationally known author of *Ringu*.

> I only lay claim to the Elisa Lam incident because I had inadvertently inspired Koji to write the story "Floating Water," which became *Dark Water*. While I myself had no hand in the tragedy, I am more than a little disturbed that something I inspired came to pass without my intervention. Perhaps fate works in stranger ways than I do. Still, I wish her nothing but peace.
>
> —From the diary of Tenebris, The Boogeyman

CHAPTER TEN

WIRED FOR WEIRD

SLENDER MAN AND THE NEW URBAN LEGEND

IT ALL BEGAN with a fire, the disappearance of fourteen children, and a series of eerie, chilling photographs. It wasn't supposed to get out of hand, but it did.

Or did it?

On the *Something Awful* web forum, a popular thread was posted by a moderator who goes by the name "Gerogerigegege." The topic posed a unique and creative challenge to the website's visitors: create an urban legend, make it as authentic and scary as possible, then leak it out onto the Internet.

Most of the stories readers came up with were rehashes of very old, time-worn folktales that had been run around the block millions of times before. Ghost babies, UFOs over Washington, Lee Harvey Oswald's alien doppelgänger . . . you get the idea.

But one entry raised more than a few eyebrows. Posted by a user going by the name "Victor Surge," the story of what happened prior to the Stirling City Library Fire of 1986 would soon become gospel in online communities. The post, dated June 8, 2009, consisted of two fairly ordinary black and white photographs and an unsettling back story of how the photos came into existence.

In the photo taken in 1983, we see a typical playground. Children are playing on the slides and swing sets. But in the background, surrounded by children, is a tall, dark, faceless figure in a black suit and tie, its long arms reaching out for the children. A swirling wave of what looks like black tentacles are emanating from its back.

141

The second photograph, taken by photographer Mary Thomas in 1986, showed another group of children—teenagers this time—flanked by the same tall, faceless being, stoically standing in the background.

In a disturbing coincidence, fourteen of the children pictured, as well as the photographer herself, disappeared a week before a disastrous fire claimed the historic Stirling City Library on June 20, 1986. The only thing connecting the two photographs—and the disappearances—was the tall, gangling being with the featureless face and off-putting height. Authorities would dismiss the notion of this purported supernatural being almost immediately, and film experts agreed that the odd thing in the photographs was most likely an anomaly on the film. For years, the quiet town of Stirling City tried to forget about this Tall Man, giving him the near-comic nickname, Slender Man. Now, he was back, and he wasn't going away so quietly this time.

This was the gist of Victor Surge's fictional urban legend, Slender Man, which stood out like a diamond in the rough, spreading its wings across the Net in victory. Soon, other users would produce "authentic" Slender Man photographs of their own. In time, the name "Victor Surge" would be lost, but the Slender Man mythos he created would only grow larger, more elaborate, and more real.

In reality, Victor Surge was a young man by the name of Eric Knudsen, a Florida native who, to this day, is still surprised at the success of the Slender Man mythos and is notoriously protective of the Slender Man copyright he holds.

By 2011, Slender Man had become a fully formed, absolutely chilling supernatural creature. Standing nearly eight feet tall with equally long arms and legs, the "tentacles" emanating from his back became razor sharp defensive tools he could use should anyone get in the way of his work. He is an Angel of Death, a reaper who takes children to the Underworld early so that they might possibly avoid a protracted, painful death. Photoshopped images of medieval woodcut drawings popped up of "Slendy," cementing his reputation as an ages-old creature. Today, he is frequently seen in a black suit and red tie, his need to appear normal betraying his outlandish exterior, which makes him unsettling and familiar at the same time.

Realistically, the Slender Man is the real-world vision of a flesh-and-blood Jack Skellington from 1993's *The Nightmare Before Christmas*. Nearly every attribute that the Slender Man claims as his own was borrowed quite liberally from the king of Halloween Town, from his long arms and legs, slithery tendrils radiating from his back and neck, and of course, the pale white head. Knudsen wisely erased Skellington's familiar jack o' lantern expression and left a chilling void in its place.

Why Slender Man spread like a disease throughout the Internet isn't too hard to figure out, for most people love a good ghost story, and in the case of Slender Man, the myth was propelled by people who had no idea he was a fictional character. While the story was obviously fiction and stated so on the *Something Awful* website, readers and horror junkies not familiar with the bizarre website came across it in other ways, often without the benefit of knowing it was pure fiction. Their spreading of the Slender Man tale resulted in an urban legend of incredible staying power that would spawn fan fiction, video games, and rumors of a Slender Man movie. Slender Man the myth is an unstoppable machine that refuses to go away quietly, yet it is good that he hasn't. In the modern world, where the Internet is live twenty-four hours a day, seven days a week, the tale of Slender Man very easily crossed over from the virtual realm and into the lives of those who put him onto a pedestal, often with horrific results.

On May 31, 2014, two twelve-year-old girls in Waukesha, Wisconsin, held down and stabbed a twelve-year-old classmate nineteen times, claiming that they did so in hopes that Slender Man would allow them to become associates of his in the Underworld. Their victim miraculously survived her wounds and was rescued by a passing cyclist after she managed to crawl to the edge of the woods near the roadside. The two twelve-year-old assailants were hastily arrested and taken to jail, charged as adults in the assault.

But the question of mental health came up when one of the girls testified in open court that she not only talked to Slender Man, but also to Lord Voldemort from the *Harry Potter* series and to one of the Teenage Mutant Ninja Turtles. Not surprisingly, she and her co-conspirator were deemed unfit to stand trial and were remanded to a state-run psychiatric hospital. By August of 2015, a judge had declared that they were finally competent to stand trial and they would do so in adult court. Their trial has yet to begin as of this writing.

Knudsen remained fairly quiet on the entire matter, even as his creation was being blamed for the girls' psychotic behavior. In a statement to the media, Knudsen said, "I am deeply saddened by the tragedy in Wisconsin, and my heart goes out to the families of those affected by this terrible act."

This brutal act of bloody assault sent a wave throughout the world, spawning similar attacks that parents and police blamed on the Slender Man. A Cincinnati woman reported her thirteen-year-old daughter to police after the girl attacked her with a knife. The unidentified girl had recently begun writing horror fiction, with Slender Man taking a starring role in several of her stories.

On September 4, 2014, a fourteen-year-old girl in Port Richey, Florida, set her family's house on fire while her mother and nine-year-old brother were inside. While Slender Man wasn't singled out specifically, the girl's obsession with him made it look fairly obvious where her interests lay.

Perhaps the most devastating act inspired by Slender Man came during an epic 2015 epidemic of suicides on the Pine Ridge Reservation, located in northern South Dakota. Authorities say that nine native youths, ranging in age between twelve and twenty-four, all committed suicide between December 2014 and April 2015. While only one of the suicides was blatantly inspired by Slender Man, it is common knowledge on the reservation that Slender Man is a powerful influence.

Chris Carey, a youth minister who worked with the kids of the Pine Ridge Reservation, told the *New York Times* in a May 1, 2015, story that: "They call him the Tall Man spirit. He's appearing to these kids and telling them to kill themselves." The Tall Man spirit could refer to some Native American legends that talk of there being a "suicide guide" similar to Slender Man, a quietly sinister being that helps aid the dishonored find peace through self-annihilation.

Today, most Slender Man tales and photos are found on a website called *Creepypasta*, a unique play on the computer savvy term "Copy and Paste." *Creepypasta* is a fairly anonymous forum for horror and science fiction writers with a flair for disturbing material. It is a site that allows the tales to be shared, copied, expanded upon, or simply enjoyed, and, like all successful creations, *Creepypasta* writers came up with more than a few Slender Man-inspired imitations, such as the ultra-creepy Jeff the Killer and the exploits of Ted the Caver.

Jeff the Killer was created by a YouTube user named "Sesseur." The video story of Jeff the Killer concerns a horribly disfigured young man who accidentally doused himself with acid while trying to clean his bathtub. The pain and torment drove Jeff insane and he cut a smile into his cheeks and burned off his eyelids. Now a thoroughly psychotic killer, Jeff sneaks into houses at night and whispers to his victims "Go to sleep" before savagely murdering them. While the original video lacks a certain panache and suffers from a skewed sense of structure, other writers and meme kings would take Jeff the Killer and make him a truly frightening example of dementia. He would soon find fame in the online world as fodder for memes and at least one creepy video game.

Ted the Caver, meanwhile, wasn't a boogeyman-type figure at all. Rather, he was written up as an amateur spelunker who documented strange paranormal activity in a very tight, very creepy cave system known as Mystery Cave. His tale began on March 23, 2001, when "Ted" posted a story of an odd series of events occurring while he and his best friends, Brad and Joe, explored the caves. The blog documents the occurrences they encountered, including ghastly screaming, unnatural wind, and strange hieroglyphics that appear deep inside the cave where no other human could have possibly been before. This was one of the first cases of the growth of an Internet legend, and it certainly predated Slender Man, though it was quite obviously inspired by *The Blair Witch Project*.

On a more personal note, my favorite of all the Internet hoaxes is the tale of The Rake. Created by a user at *4Chan*, a user-supported precursor to *Creepypasta*, the earliest known appearance of The Rake came on July 20, 2006, in a story posted on the *Something Awful* web forums by Brian Somerville. The "mythology" of The Rake was far more detailed and elaborate, as opposed to Slender Man, which could have derailed it, but instead made it soar. The Rake, a six-foot-tall humanoid with three eyes and a mouth full of tiny, dull teeth, was first spoken of in the twelfth century, appearing in different cultures of Europe, Asia, America, and Africa. While The Rake mostly observes humans in the forest from a distance, he will stand on his hind legs and attack if threatened. But he's also not afraid of humans either. He has been seen skulking around suburban homes, peering into windows and hiding in shrubbery. "Witnesses" have claimed to wake in the middle of the night in horror as The Rake looks down on them in their beds. He was so strange and odd looking that a fan-made video depicting The Rake made the news broadcast on Fort Wayne, Indiana's Channel 33 morning news. While most viewers wrote it off immediately as a hoax, it still left an indelible impression in the hearts of the morning anchors, who took it way too seriously.

But Slender Man is the Internet's chosen Boogeyman of today and in the annals of Tenebris's storied career, no other tale came as close to reality as the Slender Man. While he actively denies creating the character, he applauds Eric Knudsen's flawless attention to detail. Knudsen gave out only a tidbit of information about the photographs he'd doctored, creating a panting need for more information about this faceless creature, who may have been responsible for abducting the fourteen children pictured with him in the photos. Knudsen created a brilliant starting-off point for an urban legend, a classic tale that would be enriched and added upon by everyone who tells and re-tells the tale. In no time at all, an entire history created by a massive fanbase of horror aficionados became canon.

> Before you had angels and succubi, and then ghosts and spirits, today we have shadow people and inter-dimensional beings. The Slender Man, and other newly created entities, are just the newest addition in the progression of a long, and very real, human tradition.
>
> You've seen him, now you can't un-see him.
>
> —Eric Knudsen (Victor Surge)

WHERE DO WE GO FROM HERE?

I STOOD ON THE rotting floorboards, peering into the darkness of the old house. I stood there silently, stood there dumbfounded. Stood there feeling a bit lost.

There was no voice in my head leading me. No unnatural shadows cast against the dark interior. Six months had passed and the place seemed like a different house altogether. Gone was the forbidding fear I felt just by looking at it. Somewhere in the surrounding forest I heard the cackle of a crow and the warble of a robin. Everything in me, and everything around me, told me he was no longer here. But this is where he had instructed me to return the book, and so I did as I was told. Under my arm I clutched the old binder of his writings and I stepped inside, the floor groaning beneath me.

The air was stagnant, full of antiquity, and even when I'd made it to the basement and looked upon the coal room where we'd first met, the house just seemed dead. Dead and rotting, as if life had been drained of it centuries ago. But was it Tenebris's absence that changed the way it felt, or was it my own perspective that changed it? The chair was still overturned from before when he'd scared me out of the room the first time.

Taking in the darkness and inhaling deeply, I said, "I just wanted you to know I'm finished. It turned out pretty good, I think."

I placed the old binder on the floor next to the overturned chair and stepped back. Maybe I was hoping for an answer, but there was none. Nothing but the smell of wood decaying and the feeling of being all alone in an empty house. Sometimes you can feel the pulse of others, even when you can't see them. The energy alone magnetizes you, but here there was nothing.

"Where do we go from here?" I asked, still hoping to see his white-eyed stare or hear that rasping voice in the dark, the one that could curdle milk and make spiders run in terror.

Silence.

But as I turned to leave, I heard, ever so softly, coming from the darkness behind me, in a soft, gravelly voice . . .

"See you soon . . ."

THE BEAUTY IN TERROR, THE TERROR IN BEAUTY

HAVING SPOKEN TO him directly and seen his true face, effectively undermining his entire skill set to terrify the world, I find it fairly easy to reflect not only on who he is, but what kind of an impact he's made. Truly, The Boogeyman is more than just a story. He's a legend held bound inside a myth that will endure forever no matter the culture, location, or era. His influence on art, music, movies, and literature is solid, varied, and wide. Tenebris has managed to do what few other creatures could: he has inspired delight as well as fear, beauty as well as repulsion. Whether it be through direct, face-to-face influence, or via one of Tenebris's well-known aliases, the terror in beauty and the beauty in terror have been captured in so many different, beautiful ways that such pieces are often the most revered in the art world.

For centuries, images of horrific beings have held a spot in the popular imagination for one very good reason: we like to be scared. But the fear Tenebris brings about isn't a broad fear such as terrorism, nuclear holocaust, or mass murder. It is an innate fear, a primal terror, the same one we experience when we get on a roller coaster ride or stroll through a haunted attraction. In the early days of artistic expression, drawings were crude, almost caricature-like, yet the message came across very clearly. Ancient Egyptian, Greek, and Roman cultures made certain there was a distinction between man and beast, and the beast almost always tended to be larger than life. The Minotaur of Crete and graven images of the snake-haired Medusa spring to mind almost immediately as do the creepy depictions of Anubis, often illustrated as a dog-faced god of the dead, and Sobek, the crocodile-headed god of the Nile and fertility in Egyptian mythology.

ART

AS MEDIEVAL ART sprang to life in the eleventh and twelfth centuries, an emphasis on detail and spatial equality became more important attributes. Artists of the time, when depicting their beasts, began to draw from the beastliest of their experiences thus far: the sudden importance of the Devil in newly devout Christian lands. In the beginning, the Devil would be portrayed as a hulking, horned beast, but soon enough, old Scratch would come to embody the look of the formerly accepted, now incredibly inappropriate, Greek god known as Pan. With the legs and hoofs of a goat and the monstrous upper body of a dusky sailor, the medieval Devil was designed from the start as a smack in the face to the gods of old, who had been replaced by the Christian God and Jesus Christ. Engravings, etchings, woodcuts, and paintings in all mediums have been preserved showing Satan in this form, dragging hapless sinners through the yawning gates of Hell to face an eternity of damnation. But as time went by, and more people paid increasing attention to the Book of Revelations, the Devil began to change again, this time taking on the fearsome, and more appropriate, look of a multi-headed dragon rising from the sea.

But it wasn't just Satan who was portrayed in such a way. Legends of the time, from the Loup Garou to the Strigoi and Baba Yaga all found a place in artistic expression. Let's face it: everyone loves a good monster, especially when it can make your blood run cold and your heart race. Endorphins and adrenaline are good things indeed. Its the reason newspapers sold, why museums were created, and why artists became artists. The feeling a piece of art creates in someone is priceless, especially when confronted by that which we fear most.

Such was the case of Francisco Goya, whose career as a brilliant painter took a haunting twist near the end of his life. Goya, a Spaniard who once worked as the official painter in the court of King Charles IV of Spain, found his life to be almost unbearable by the time he reached his seventy-fifth birthday. Consumed by the fear of his own insanity and facing his own mortality, Goya painted what are now known as "The Black Paintings." Originally painted on black backgrounds on the walls of his home in Madrid as a gigantic mural, The Black Paintings were removed from the walls and carefully transferred onto canvas almost fifty years after Goya's death in 1828. His two-story home literally had almost every single wall filled with intense, dark images and baleful, almost melancholic faces. Of the fourteen paintings, two stand out as brilliant examples of The Boogeyman's influence: that of the disturbing and grisly *Saturn Devouring His Son*, and the vision of a witches coven at work, *Witches' Sabbath*.

Saturn Devouring His Son depicts the Roman god devouring one of his sons whole. The story, according to Roman mythology, revolves around the god Saturn becoming suspicious of his children. He was afraid that they were conspiring to steal his throne from him, so he devoured them all before they had the opportunity to usurp him. Obviously, this image reminds us of The Boogeyman as a child eater or child stealer, as the son Saturn is consuming is no bigger than a newborn baby. What madness drove Goya to paint this particular image first is up for debate, but one has to wonder if perhaps he suspected his own children of trying to manipulate or deceive him.

Witches' Sabbath, likewise, also explores these same themes of violence, intimidation, aging, and death as the Devil, in the form of a shrouded goat, presides over a coven of ugly and terrified witches. Of all the things in the painting, it is the vision of a young girl who stands clearly apart from the proceedings, as if she is aghast and abhorred to be present. Witches were a common theme for Goya, as evidenced by his earlier painting, *Witches Flight* (1797–1798) and the similarly titled, *Witches Sabbath* (1798). At first sight, it would seem that Goya presents the witches not as independent spell casters acting alone, but as instruments of Satan who perform their magic only at his behest and in his honor, a grossly inaccurate generalization. But it is in that generalization that one should see the satire of the piece, a slight jab in the ribs with a crowbar at the Spanish Inquisition and the ghastly witch trials, mocking the medieval fear politicians and religious figures often used to secure followers and repress individual thought.

The other pieces in the collection, while not as overtly Boogey-ish, spoke volumes about his uncertainty of people. Even in paintings of old men doing nothing but eating soup, Goya paints his subjects with a mistrusting hand, leaving behind a darkness in them that bleeds with uneasiness. The Black Paintings collectively are a rare and haunting portrait of burgeoning madness captured at its inception. Currently, all of the so-called Black Paintings are held in the Museo del Prado in Madrid, Spain, but you, dear reader, may view them all at the following website: www.franciscodegoya.net.

In similar fashion and predating Goya's best work by nearly ten years, Swiss artist Henry Fuseli's *The Nightmare* (1781) manages to capture both the horror of oppressed sleep and the fierce repression of sexuality all in one breathtaking brush stroke. Fuseli had a knack for the bizarre and the haunted; many of his paintings depicted monstrous creatures, mythic warriors, and vengeful gods. But it is *The Nightmare* that earned Fuseli his golden ticket into immortality. The painting was so popular that Fuseli would often paint and repaint duplicate versions of the same painting to sell to art collectors of the time. Engravings and etchings popped up everywhere. *The Nightmare* by Fuseli was the 1781 equivalent of The Beatles crossing Abbey Road, or perhaps even Marilyn Monroe's dress blowing upward in *The Seven Year Itch*. It depicts a sleeping, supine lady in a sheer white night gown with an impish demon sitting on her chest as a white-eyed horse pokes its head through the curtains of her bed chamber. The Imp, also called an Incubus and the horse (or mare) bring back to mind the ideal images of nightmares in folklore, specifically the tale of "The Mare," which the horse represents but only in name. The Nordic tale of "The Mare" tells of a demon who would seep into the dreams of the sleeping. The Incubus, meanwhile, is known as a very potent, very aggressive sexual demon who invades the dreams of women in order to have sex with them. A female version of the Incubus, known as the Succubus, is said to invade the dreams of men so that they may bear demonic children together whether he wants to or not. While *The Nightmare* is Fuseli's most recognized work, it certainly is not his only contribution to the art world, and his style is said to have influenced everyone from John Constable and William Etty, as well as the brilliant artist and poet, William Blake, whose own work owes more than a reasonable debt of gratitude to Fuseli's bizarre imagery. For many, it was *The Nightmare* that opened our eyes to the dark beauty of grandiose art, proving that a terrifying dream could indeed be captured for all eternity in one single painting. Today, *The Nightmare* can be found on permanent display in the Detroit Institute of Arts in Michigan.

As for William Blake, his stunning watercolor interpretations of *The Beast of Revelations* for an illustrated version of The Bible stand out as his most famous works, primarily due to their inclusion in the plot line of Thomas Harris's *Red Dragon* in which the villain takes his dangerous obsession with Blake's Red Dragon to murderous extremes. In a series of four watercolor paintings, William Blake illustrated *The Great Red*

Dragon to startlingly powerful effect, most exquisitely in *The Great Red Dragon and the Woman Clothed in Sun*, in which the spectacularly tall Red Dragon stands over a passive woman embroiled in the rays of the sun, its muscular tail winding about her body. It is —without question—the sexiest vision of the Devil that has ever been rendered. But Blake was known primarily for his eloquent poetry and prose, not for his artistic merits; many of Blake's peers and the adoring public quietly denied the beauty of his painted works, yet still bought them up willingly. Of course, it wouldn't be until much later that his brilliance with watercolors would be appreciated. Like Goya, William Blake's darker material came near the end of his life as he illustrated versions of *The Divine Comedy*, *The Canterbury Tales*, and, of course, *The Holy Bible*. While *The Great Red Dragon and the Woman Clothed in Sun* can be found at the Brooklyn Museum in New York City, the other three paintings in the series are housed at the National Gallery of Art in Washington, DC, and at the Rosenbach Museum and Library in Philadelphia, Pennsylvania.

One of the lesser known artists of the early 1900s, but no less important, was that of Austrian-born Alfred Leopold Isidor Kubin (1877–1959), a poet and artist, like Blake, whose darker inclinations made him the perfect choice for illustrating books by Edgar Allan Poe, E. T. A. Hoffmann, and Fyodor Dostoyevsky. His early techniques drew upon a rather broad swath of *avant garde* expressionism, but as he grew older, his work became more reality based with just enough of that old *avant garde* to keep the viewer on edge. Kubin was a reclusive, depressed man for most of his life, and his mortality was always nearby in his thoughts ever since he attempted suicide standing over the grave of his mother in 1896. He drew and painted images of mythical manticores, water serpents, and the morbid hanging deaths of proper women. While many of his paintings and his reputation became lost to all but the smallest circles of art fanatics, his terrifying masterpiece *The Spectre of the Sea* (also known as *The Water Ghost*) has become renowned the world over for its stark portrayal of a boat lost at sea in the midst of a torrential, dark storm. The crew's plight is amplified by the presence of a skeletal ghoul cloaked in black rising from the sea, dwarfing their boat as waves rise up and crash around them.

But Devils and demons aren't all that The Boogeyman inspired. Truly, Tenebris's reach was never more evident than in the works of more contemporary artists. However, his influence was felt in a more humorous vein than before. Indeed, The Boogeyman's legacy was taken up by people who not only understood him but felt a kinship to him, as if they understood the darkness better than he. Whereas other artists accentuated the fear The Boogeyman instilled in others, artists like Charles

Addams, Edward Gorey, and Maurice Sendak chose to accentuate the giddy thrills of fear as well as the harmless nature of folklore and stories of monsters in the night.

With the creation of The Addams Family cartoon for *The New Yorker* magazine, Charles Addams began a legacy of morbid rib-tickling antics that would continue to inspire artists, filmmakers, and authors well after his death in 1988. His Morticia and Gomez Addams were the perfect foils for the ideal nuclear family, a lambasting of the *Leave It To Beaver* ethos that many took way too seriously. While the Addams Family were a curious lot, there is no doubt that they loved each other in their own special way and got their kicks in equally unique ways as well, usually at the expense of the "squares." And the family came complete with not one, but several boogeymen: Uncle Fester, the cue-ball headed master of disaster; Lurch, the Frankenstein's Monster-esque butler; and Cousin Itt, a four-foot-tall gibberish-spouting, walking carpet of immaculately straight hair that always seemed to be in place at all times.

Edward Gorey took Addams's darkly humorous approach even farther with his bizarre illustrations of horrible things following after normal people. Gorey began his career in fun-fear in 1953 when he began illustrating modern classics such as *Dracula* and *War of the Worlds*, establishing his legendary style of sparsely used pen-and-ink, exaggerated bodies, and over the top punch lines. But at his heart, Gorey was a sensational surrealist, crafting odd worlds on blank pages. He was one of the first to create the wordless story book, crafting an entire, cohesive narrative using only his artwork. In time, his unique style and oddball endeavors garnered him the praise and admiration of the Gothic community, who held him on high as one of their most astounding and important artists.

Like Edward Gorey, Maurice Sendak had a flair for the dark side but chose to embrace what he saw as the silliness of it instead, using the monsters of faraway lands to empower children to be themselves no matter the situation. Of course, I speak of his classic children's book, 1963's *Where the Wild Things Are*. It tells the tale of a young boy named Max who is sent to his room without supper for acting out while dressed in a wolf costume. While there, he is transported to a mystical island where there are nothing but very tall, very monstrous-looking "Wild Things" who revere Max as their new leader because he proves himself to be the wildest of them all. But Max opts to go home, much to the dismay of the Wild Things, and finds a hot supper waiting for him. The book was banned and panned at first, mostly because parents found the Wild Things to be shocking and scary, while some believed Sendak excused Max's incorrigible behavior. But children know more then adults give them credit for; they saw the power and the value of having confidence in yourself in the prose and pictures of the book and the book was constantly being checked out of libraries. Eventually, the critics and parents came around and realized how amazing the book was, for it didn't pander to children. It treated them as humans with real feelings and genuine emotional needs. This was one of Sendak's greatest gifts as an illustrator and writer: he knew how to talk *to* kids, not down to them.

I'll wind down this section on artists who brilliantly captured the essence of The Boogeyman by asking your indulgence as I salute my own favorite children's book, *The King with Six Friends*, beautifully written by Jay Williams and illustrated by the magnificent Imero Gobbato. While not overtly influenced by The Boogeyman, Williams and Gobbato wisely chose fearsome creatures and objects to prove the point that fear only gets in the way of moving forward and being a good person. The book concerns the adventures of an exiled king named Zar who sets out to find a new kingdom to rule. On the way, he meets a series of odd friends who, at first, seem scary as they are in the guise of other things. There is Edge, a man who has been transformed into an ax and left wedged in a downed tree; Agus, a man who is first seen as an elephant being terrorized by a mouse before Zar rescues him; Kindle, a spritely fellow rescued by Zar in the form of a smoldering fire in the rain; Eryx, a man transformed into a snake that had found itself tied in a knot before Zar untangled him; Furze, a tree who became a man once Zar removed a nest of pesky birds from his branches; and Dumble, a bee who became human once more after Zar rescued him from the hungry clutches of a honey-stealing bear. While all of these creatures could have turned back into humans to save themselves, doing so would have disrupted or destroyed the lives of others around them. Only with the help of kind King Zar could the friends become human once more and not hurt anything or anyone else. Together, the King with his six friends found their kingdom and worked together to make it awesome, using their unique skills as a team to accomplish the seemingly impossible. The narrative is a classic example of true fairy tale storytelling and the artwork is mystical, fun, and inspiring. It also happens to encourage the empowerment of children (which is something Tenebris sought to do with his nightly excursions,) to encourage them to see the good in everything, and that everyone in the world has at least one special gift.

MUSIC

A S IN PAINTING, the world of symphonies and other expressions of music are ripe with Boogeyman-influenced palettes of terror.

Horror is, without a doubt, one of the easier emotions to convey, whether it be on a stretched canvas, performed by a 100-piece orchestra, or laid out by five guys with guitars and keyboards. Horror, like romance, touches upon several different triggers within us; we've all felt the pangs of both romance and horror sometime in our lives. Sometimes we feel the horror of romance, and sometimes it is the romance of horror we feel.

Classical music, of course, always came first, yet only a few composers have managed to pull off the fantastic and the horrific. French composer Hector Berlioz (1803–1869), for one, was responsible for creating one of the most intricate and mesmerizing pieces of music in history, the *Symphonie Fantastique*. Written in five movements, the score tells the story of a frustrated artist who has overdosed on opium while mourning the death of love in his life. While the opium does not kill him, it does provide horrifying hallucinatory visions in a dream-like state. While every piece of the symphony is brilliant and beautiful in its own right, it is the final movement, "Dream of the Night of the Sabbath," that tends to garner much of the acclaim, due mostly in part to Stanley Kubrick's use of it as the opening music for his film *The Shining*. Brooding and full of despair, the piece complements The Boogeyman perfectly as he slinks out from under the bed and into our nightmares.

Night on Bald Mountain, like the *Symphonie Fantastique*, was a "musical picture" of a witches' Sabbath that culminates with the arrival of Old Scratch himself, the Devil. Written by Russian composer Modest Mussorgsky (1839–1881) in 1867, it was generally dismissed by his colleagues and mentors, who refused to perform it. Understandably, the piece at the time was lacking proper structure and vision, but all the makings of a brilliant symphony were there. It wasn't until fellow Russian composer Nikolai Rimsky-Korsakov rearranged the work five years after Mussorgsky's death that the famous tone poem was accepted as the brilliant piece that it was. There are many who debate the validity of Mussorgsky's work, critics who place far too much credit on Rimsky-Korsakov's doorstep and far too little on the hard work of Mussorgsky.

But when it comes to horrific tone poems with a hint of fantasy and more than a dash of romanticism, no one captured a night in the graveyard better than French composer Camille Saint-Saëns (1835–1921) and his magical *Danse Macabre*. Set in a graveyard on Halloween night, the piece begins with Death calling the dead out of their graves with his fiddle as the music of nightmares causes them to dance and waltz until the macabre party is silenced by the break of dawn, and the dead return to their graves for another year. But like all masterful creations, it was hardly appreciated in its own time as critics ripped Saint Saëns a new one over the use of a screeching fiddle to signify Death, and the presence of a xylophone to emulate skeletons dancing. Taken from the old French tales of how Death would come on Halloween to summon forth the dead for one night only, *Danse Macabre* became one of the first tone poems to directly reflect French folklore.

The macabre tone poem was a sort of rite of passage for many composers, especially for those listed prior as well as Franz Liszt, Ludwig Van Beethoven, and even Wolfgang Amadeus Mozart, whose dark and brooding Don Giovanni had all the aspects of a tone poem but was written as a full-length opera. These pieces of music shine a light on the darkness in all of us and remind us of simpler times, of trembling fears foolishly hidden beneath Victorian clothes and wigs. Its hardly a wonder at all that the macabre nature of that particular brand of classical music would be picked up and celebrated by the Gothic sub-culture in the late 1990s and early 2000s.

With the advent of synthesizers and computers, entire scores could be composed, arranged, and performed by only one or two people. It afforded those with talent to write, perform, record, and market their music in the way in which they wanted. Called "New Age music" today, performers and bands like Mike Oldfield, Yes, David Arkenstone, Philip Glass, and Kitaro found great success by doing all the work themselves with very little input from the outside. In truth, New Age music evokes a holistic, mystical feeling that tries to reach toward some sort of musical nirvana, and a journey is almost always taken when one takes the time to listen.

But just as there are those who search for light inside music, there are those who feel more comfortable in the darkness, which is why bands like Nox Arcana and Midnight Syndicate flourish in both the New Age and Gothic subcultures.

Midnight Syndicate was initially formed in 1996 by Edward Douglas, a composer and filmmaker hailing from Chardon, Ohio. The first pieces of Midnight Syndicate music were composed by Douglas for a low-budget horror film he'd recently completed, *The Dead Matter*, and Midnight Syndicate was born. Teaming up with fantasy artist Joseph Vargo and composer Gavin Goszka, Midnight Syndicate re-created dark classical music by basing their pieces of Vargo's artwork and on movies that didn't exist. What resulted was a *tour-de-force* of pulse-pounding horror and fantasy that immediately changed the attitude of the Halloween industry. No longer would haunted attractions have to recycle John Carpenter's played-out "Halloween Theme" over and over. Here was a group of men who set out to deliberately exploit the darkness and they did it well. Midnight Syndicate still records to day, though they recently began to explore other holidays with their music, most notably with 2015's *Christ-*

mas: A Ghostly Gathering. Midnight Syndicate have since embraced the Halloween industry and occasionally will perform expensive live shows complete with special effects, pyrotechnics, and interactive audience participation areas.

Nox Arcana was formed in 2003 by former Midnight Syndicate member Joseph Vargo and William Piotrowski. Essentially, Vargo sought to produce the same type of music he'd been exposed to in Midnight Syndicate and, along with his partner Piotrowski, he did so rather well, creating plush soundscapes of absolute horror that mingled well with a dark sense of whimsy. Meaning "mysteries of the night" in Latin, Nox Arcana drew in rabid supporters who responded to their story-driven instrumental recordings. Nox Arcana's ghostly *Darklore Manor* captures the essence of a Gothic haunted house tale perfectly, while their *Carnival of Lost Souls* manages to entice and terrify us with everything that was scary about circus acts and carnivals in general. Over the course of twelve years, Nox Arcana has released twenty-three albums of horror- and fantasy-inspired recordings. Like Midnight Syndicate, Nox Arcana travel the same path, but tend to keep their goals a shade more grounded with their music and art, opting to celebrate the season and the music rather than over-commercialize it.

> Nox Arcana . . . I like them. It's feel-good music played beautifully. Reminds me of Lover's Lane a little.
>
> —Tenebris, The Boogeyman

But let's be honest: The Boogeyman was made for rock 'n' roll music. He isn't nice, he isn't pleasant, and he's fairly anti-social, most of the time—just like good rock 'n' roll music should be. And like rock 'n' roll music, The Boogeyman only seems to be appreciated by the youth and those enlightened enough to respect him. Of course, early blues musicians and singers like Screamin' Jay Hawkins and Robert Johnson invoked the power of The Boogeyman for their music quite often, while big band leaders like Henry Hall provided ways to avoid The Boogeyman. Novelty songs of the '50s and '60s, like "The Purple People Eater," "Monster Mash," and "The Cockroach That Ate Cincinnati" were all the rage, but only managed to make fun of the boogeyman and all his forms instead of revere him.

It wasn't until bands like Black Sabbath, Coven, Comus, Black Widow, and Blue Oyster Cult erupted in the late '60s and early '70s that Tenebris got the attention he deserved. But even as those bands used monsters and dark tales to influence their lyrics and music, most of the time the subject would be re-routed around Tenebris and be more about the Devil.

The Boogeyman was cute.

The Devil was terrifying, and people took the Devil seriously.

But not all rock stars idolized or placed the Devil onto a pedestal. There were a few who remained fixated on monsters and did their best to revere them in song. One of the first and possibly the greatest theatrical madmen in rock history to do so was Alice Cooper, who at first claimed his name was pulled from a séance with a Ouija BoardTM, but later claimed he chose it because it just sounded witchy. Alice Cooper the band and later on Alice Cooper the singer reveled in tales of monsters, the dark side, and of scary horrifying things but managed to temper those hard-edged subjects with an obvious case of tongue-in-cheek humor. "I Love The Dead" and "Cold Ethyl" managed to make necrophilia sound almost fun, while "The Ballad of Dwight Frye" and "Steven" brought the chilling effects of madness to the forefront. But it was the songs "Welcome to My Nightmare," "Feed My Frankenstein," and "Roses on White Lace" that really paid proper tribute to the big bad monster in the closet.

Roky Ericksen was a founding member and songwriter for the psychedelic '60s band the 13th Floor Elevators. But a diagnosis of paranoid schizophrenia and a penchant for hallucinatory drug use landed him in a mental hospital in 1968. When he emerged four years later, his damaged mind focused mainly on the dark ideas of horror, science fiction, and fairy tales. By the time he resumed writing songs in the 1980s, his brilliant songwriting, eerie voice, and gift for bluesy playing would call to mind the most horrible of all The Boogeyman's tales while placing a sheen of beauty atop them at the same time. In songs like "Two Headed Dog," "Night of the Vampire," "I Walked with a Zombie," and "Burn the Flames," he manages to balance B-movie kitsch and ethereal, epic poetry like a master. Roky Ericksen sings his songs like he has nothing to lose, as if he's singing for his life, as if Hell Hounds will catch him if he stops, bringing out a haunting urgency with every note he plays and every chord he strums. Roky seems to have conquered his demons and today enjoys a fairly respected cult following in tighter musical circles who recognize his true genius.

Of course, Alice Cooper and Roky Ericksen's success led to a plethora of homages from other artists, most of them fairly forgettable knock-off's that never really hit it big. But one act that did, Los Angeles metal band Lizzy Borden, took Alice Cooper's theatrical menace and shot it full of steroids, creating a musical and theatrical experience unlike any other band that had come before it. Led by lead singer Lizzy Borden, the band managed to avoid pretty much every cliché of the popular glam metal music of the time. Granted, they wrote about sex just as much as Mötley Crüe, Ratt, and Poison, but it was tempered with violence, horror, and madness. In doing so, they became one of the few shock rock bands to flourish in the decadent '80s metal scene. Their concerts were more like dark rides at the carnival than the traditional house party on the Sunset Strip. They were also one of the first metal bands to write a song about Caligula, Rome's own boogeyman and former emperor (1987's "Notorious") who was known for his love of murder, incest, and torture. The band's forte lies in accurately describing the things that live in the dark and the arousal the darkness provides for some, as evidenced in songs like "Flesh Eater," "Godiva," "Lord of the Flies," "Appointment with Death," and "Love You to Pieces."

If Lizzy Borden accentuated Alice Cooper's giddy goriness and penchant for theatrics, then Marilyn Manson amplified Cooper's flair for dark sexuality, though in the beginning, Manson and his band tended to cast a light upon the Boogeymen that walked around us during the day, hidden inside all of us like a dirty secret. Drug abuse, incest, the ability (and inability) to fit in, and the maddening delights of youth all are cast in a kind of sewage-soaked film, dried out, and placed in front of us. For Marilyn Manson, the boogeyman was anything that tried to keep you from being who you are, whether that be parents, friends, religious figures, or even your own self. Most often during live shows and in his beautifully disturbing music videos, Manson himself became that which he, and most of those who ever opposed him, all feared, unafraid of being the man everyone on the outside was terrified of because none of them had ever sought to understand the traumas and tribulations that drove his artistic inclinations.

Dani Filth, lead singer of the British metal band Cradle of Filth, would see similar results in his career as a metal visionary, though his interests were far closer to that of classic Lovecraftian monsters, Victorian ghost stories, and creepy tales of haunted forests and castles. Initially, Cradle of Filth played up the notion of being overtly anti-Christian, a staple for many bands in the black metal genre. But recently, the band has focused more on the romanticism of monsters, horror, and sex, substituting speed and screeching, for atmosphere and composition, making them the closest living tribute to The Boogeyman that there has ever been. Featuring albums such as *The Manticore and Other Horrors*, *Cruelty and The Beast* (based on Hungarian BoogeyWOMAN, Elizabeth Bathory), and *Midian* (based on the legendary home of monsters from Clive Barker's novella, *Cabal*.) Cradle of Filth's music now bears little resemblance to their music of then, sustaining a beautiful classical romanticism within a maelstrom of graveyard horror and frighteningly precise heavy metal, a switch that has divided many of their fans. But, like Tenebris himself, they do what they do and if you like it, come aboard. If not, get out of the way.

If we're going to discuss music of The Boogeyman, we can't forget about the black metal genre that has taken over much of the Scandinavian world. Dimmu Borgir, Black Throne, Immortal, Mayhem, and the legendary Mercyful Fate are all prime examples of bands that embrace their Scandinavian past and use the mythology of Tenebris's homeland in their music. Dimmu Borgir even took their name from Tenebris's birth land, the infamous Dimmuborgir Lava Fields in Iceland. Most believe that the black metal genre exists merely to undermine Christianity's influence, which is only part of it. As a whole, the black metal genre is a punch to the guts of Christians intent on demonizing a colorful and vivid history of Scandinavian folklore. It is an answer to the constant bashing and beating that Christianity doles out to lifestyles deemed "unholy" or "pagan-like." In reality, the lore of the Nordic countries is older and more refined than the Christian religion with a strong emphasis on taking personal responsibility for one's own actions rather than declaring said actions to be the work of the Devil or other sinister influences.

And then there is the overtly Boogey-ish. The heavy metal mascot. The oldest of them all appears to be Black Sabbath's Henry, a devilish version of fellow Brit band (and main Black Sabbath rival) Led Zeppelin. Debuting in 1975, Henry has become a more subdued mascot of late, but his image can still be found on a good number of Black Sabbath albums and merchandise. Motorhead's Snaggletooth, a disembodied, tusk-mouthed beastie appeared on their first album back in 1977. Snaggletooth would be joined by the Misfits' Crimson Skull in 1979, Iron Maiden's iconic Eddie the Head in 1980, and Megadeth's Vic Rattlehead in 1985. New York thrash band Overkill entered the mascot fray with their winged-skull hellion Chaly, a mascot aggro-metal band Avenged Sevenfold would blatantly rip-off for themselves twenty years later. Dangerous Toys, a hard rock outfit from Texas, introduced the world to a fang-toothed clown with no name in 1989.

Most of the mascots would share many things in common, the most notable being a completely fearsome and brutal appearance that surely warned the listener of what was to come once the needle dropped onto the vinyl. These creatures of fear and power evoked the spirit of the boogeyman rather well and also tended to help sell even more albums. For the most part, the Boogey-ish metal mascots have taken a backseat as of late, yet Iron Maiden's Eddie the Head is still put front and center on most everything with Maiden's name on it.

My personal favorite has been and always will be Mötley Crüe's Allister Fiend, a hairy-knuckled, swarthy beast with a penchant for scythes, pentagrams, scalpels, and brunettes. Conceived by bassist and founder Nikki Sixx, Allister Fiend embodies the best traits of each band member as well as the collectively dangerous attitude of the band itself. When tossed into the blender, each attribute helped to create a beast of a Boogeyman that still watches over the band and its fans today. Allister debuted in 1983 as the narrator of "In The Beginning . . ." from the bands *Shout at the Devil* album and soon enough, he became a fixture on T-shirts and posters. Allister even got his own video game, starring in the Mötley Crüe-themed video pinball game for the Sega game system, *Crueball*.

LITERATURE

THERE IS NO form of art more ripe with monsters than literature. But lets face it: Boogeymen were better back in the day, when they didn't sparkle and when they had no conscience. Or, perhaps it was even scarier when the monster *did* have a conscience. Mary Wollstonecraft Shelley's *Frankenstein*, for example, presented us with a beast that never asked to be born and found only pain and torment when he searched for love and acceptance. The horror of Frankenstein comes not from the Monster himself, but from the way he is treated by others. While his intentions are good at the beginning, it is we, the normal people, who turn him into the monster by exiling and humiliating him for what he looks like rather than for what he does. When his good intentions are cast aside and revealed, he is left with only with the unmitigated anger of being shunned for something he cannot help. He is a classic tormented monster who lives with the fact that no one will see the good in him if they can see his face. I believe that the eternal question in the minds of all humans—What is the meaning of life?—is hidden in every word of this particular book. Shelley philosophizes and agonizes over this question, and in the end, the answer is quite clear. Her Monster learns more about the nature of humanity in his few years alive than most anyone who is able to live out their entire lives. The dark nature of her monster is not the darkness within us, he *is* us. In one of the most terrifying passages ever written, Shelley describes how Victor Frankenstein and his monstrous creation first met. It is a passage Tenebris was insistent I include here as it accurately describes how often he is greeted. In turn, I include it here simply because it is my favorite passage from one of my favorite books.

> But it was in vain: I slept, indeed, but I was disturbed by the wildest dreams. I thought I saw Elizabeth, in the bloom of health, walking in the streets of Ingolstadt. Delighted and surprised, I embraced her; but as I imprinted the first kiss on her lips, they became livid with the hue of death; her features appeared to change, and I thought

that I held the corpse of my dead mother in my arms; a shroud enveloped her form, and I saw the grave-worms crawling in the folds of the flannel. I started from my sleep with horror; a cold dew covered my forehead, my teeth chattered, and every limb became convulsed: when, by the dim and yellow light of the moon, as it forced its way through the window shutters, I beheld the wretch—the miserable monster whom I had created. He held up the curtain of the bed and his eyes, if eyes they may be called, were fixed on me. His jaws opened, and he muttered some inarticulate sounds, while a grin wrinkled his cheeks. He might have spoken, but I did not hear; one hand was stretched out, seemingly to detain me, but I escaped, and rushed down stairs. I took refuge in the courtyard belonging to the house which I inhabited; where I remained during the rest of the night, walking up and down in the greatest agitation, listening attentively, catching and fearing each sound as if it were to announce the approach of the demoniacal corpse to which I had so miserably given life."

—Mary Wollstonecraft Shelley, *Frankenstein*, Chapter 5

While Mary Shelley may have been the first to write a monster story that became the first popular example of written horror, she wasn't the last, obviously. Very soon after the birth of *Frankenstein*, an unspoken partnership developed that would continue on to this very day. John Polidori, a doctor and attendant to the deranged Lord Byron, would pen his own horror story around the same time Mary Shelley did, a tale focusing on the vampire. In his book, *The Vampyre* (1819), we are presented the tale of Lord Ruthven and his companion, Aubrey, who share the secret of Ruthven's life as a vampire in London. Incredibly influential, Polidori's *The Vampyre* would revolutionize the vampire genre of horror fiction, not only influencing *Bram Stoker's Dracula* (which came nearly eighty years after Polidori's tale had been published) but also the entire arc of vampire lore to come, including the Twilight books and films. Interestingly enough, both *Frankenstein* and *The Vampyre* were conceived during the same summer at the same Geneva, Switzerland, estate of Lord Byron; they were the two best-known pieces of literature to come from an informal contest to see who could come up with the best ghost story. In the end, Lord Byron, a thirty-one-year-old misogynist and brilliant poet, was shown up by the eighteen-year-old mistress of Percy Shelley. Today, it is hard not to include *The Vampyre* in a conversation about *Frankenstein's* Monster.

Up until then, horror fiction was polite almost to a fault. While the tales of monsters and madmen were incredibly well written, the edges were smooth and polished, crafted for gentlemen and ladies. But a renaissance of horror fiction inspired by The Boogeyman came about first in the 1890s with the publication of Arthur Machen's *The Great God Pan* and, in 1906, with Algernon Blackwood's *The Empty House and Other Ghost Stories*. Machen's *The Great God Pan* concerns Dr. Raymond, whose main goal in life is to open the minds of man so that all may experience everything the world has to offer, a rite he calls "seeing the god Pan." What ensues is a labyrinthine maze of horrors, horrific nightmares, and the emergence of a half-human/half-beast creature that turns out to be the offspring of a god. Machen uses the medium to plumb the depths of horror by tapping into some of our most primal fears and then clobbering us with them.

While Machen was an expert at tugging at the cerebellum to garner his scares, Algernon Blackwood was more of a traditional horror story writer, focusing on truly frightening ghost stories that seemed to be almost too good to be true. His tale "The Singular Death of Morton" would be Blackwood's only foray into vampire lore, while "The Strange Adventures of a Private Secretary in New York" and "The Camp of The Dog" would show his prowess at writing werewolf tales, a favorite obsession of Tenebris, and ones truly inspired by Mr. Boogey himself. But Blackwood's shining star was hitched to his uncanny ability to scare us with ghosts, demons, and odd strangers. He knew that, and man, did he run with it.

Of course, the influence of Machen and Blackwood was infectious and many fly-by-night writers tried unsuccessfully to ape their prosperity, many times with disastrous results. But there was one writer who never tried to mimic their success; rather, he took inspiration in their abilities to create other worlds to craft his own. In time, the fantastic universe Howard Philips Lovecraft fashioned would tower over that of Machen and Blackwood and change the way monster tales were written forever. Of course, Lovecraft would never see the critical or commercial praise for his work; geniuses tend to be overlooked at first or written off completely during their lifetimes. But Lovecraft did something truly extraordinary. He was the first to create an entire, incredibly detailed alternate universe, filled with tentacled monsters, creepy crawlies, ironclad rules for their existence, and a detailed history of how they came into being. Lovecraft never had much of a chance to properly connect his stories together in the universe he envisioned; his untimely death from intestinal cancer at age forty-six and his near-poverty level financial status prevented him from doing anything other than paying the bills with whatever stories he could sell. It wasn't until after his death that a colleague of his, August Derleth, collected all of his fantastic stories and expanded the universe Lovecraft had begun into one of monstrous proportions. Known as *The Cthulhu Mythos*, it surmised that there was an alternate universe in which old gods roamed and waited for their opportunity to escape into our world, causing as much destruction and horror as possible. The water god Cthulhu is arguably the most well known and was described by Lovecraft as being like an enormous octopus with the shared attributes of both men and dragons. Lovecraft's genius lay in his fierce determination to make the world of Cthulhu as real as possible, and his dedication to this world continues to inspire card games, video games, and fantasy novels of every kind. In fact, it's fairly reasonable to assume that *The Cthulhu Mythos* is now more well known than the man who created it. Which is sad. Very sad.

One of my favorite horror novels came in 1981 from novelist Edward Levy. *The Beast Within* would be made into a gore-filled B movie (not that there's anything wrong with that) within a year of its release, but the film bore little resemblance to the actual novel, which, to me, is one of the most frightening ever written. Ever. Like, scarier than anything Stephen King ever wrote or dreamed of writing. *The Beast Within* begins with lonely housewife Sarah Scruggs, her abusive husband, Henry, and a traveling salesman by the name of Billy Connors. When Henry discovers Sarah and Billy have been sleeping together, he subjects Billy to a grueling, hellish twenty-year-long punishment. Chained in an unescapable basement and fed a steady diet of rats, garbage, and human flesh, Connors is robbed of his humanity as the titular beast within comes out. He devolves into a creature that is less than human. When Connors escapes, he creeps into the lives of unsuspecting couple Eli and Carolyn McCleary, changing them forever. What follows is a lurid, engrossing, sometimes bizarre, and thoroughly frightening take on werewolf lore that has yet to be matched. Levy did an amazing job of bringing me into the story, into Connors' world, and leaving me there.

> "Ahh, one of my favorites, too. I remember him. I watched him as he wrote that one. I only read one paragraph and left him be. If he was writing something like *that*, there was nothing I could do to scare him. I was a bit jealous of him on that one, though."
> —Tenebris, The Boogeyman

Levy's novel is, of course, a perfect example of the resurgence of the pulp horror novel in the 1980s and the glorious return of truly frightening monsters. Stephen King, Peter Straub, and Robert Bloch had made horror profitable again and publishing houses clamored to cash in. What resulted were stacks and stacks of exploitative, violent, lurid, and soundly gory tomes filled with as much sex as there was blood. Many writers missed the point of the horror novel, yet there were some who actually seemed to get it. Those few would rightfully be remembered by fans for generations to come and would influence as many new writers as King and Straub have.

Richard Laymon, one of the best pulp novelists of the era, was the author of nearly fifty novels, yet it was his first book, 1980's *The Cellar*, that remains firmly planted in my favorites column even after all these years. The book concerns a family of horrific beasts who roam the underground tunnels beneath an old dark house the locals lovingly refer to as The Beast House. The twisted history behind the house and the beasts who live there is enough to give you chills upon your chills, but what is most intoxicating is Laymon's offhand, pitch-black sense of humor mingling with the cold horror he serves up. His underground beasts, lurking in the dark seeking human flesh to not only eat but also to plunder, is the stuff of nightmares.

But if there were any writers who made accepting The Boogeyman as the beautiful creature he was, it was Ray Bradbury and Richard Matheson, two writers who revolutionized the modern horror novel while also introducing some of the eeriest Boogeymen ever committed to the page. While Bradbury specialized in science fiction and fantasy, he was quite adept at writing horror as well, as evidenced by his sublime novella, *Something Wicked This Way Comes* (1962). Here, The Boogeyman takes the form of a mysterious carnival owner named Mr. G. M. Dark, who may just be the Devil. He is the classic Illustrated Man, with tattoos covering his body, one for each soul he's stolen. As the proprietor of Cooger and Dark's Pandemonium Circus and Sideshow, Mr. Dark exudes true menace as he searches out souls of the people of Green Town, Illinois. The innocent, virginal Green Town is seen as being infiltrated by the hellish carnival folk, an act akin to some kind of demonic seduction or rape, where the promise of dreams made real came at a very high cost. What is interesting is that, during the cynical 1960s in which it was written, *Something Wicked This Way Comes* extols a beauty about simple small-town life, the purity of youth, and the power of love among best friends and between a father and son.

Richard Matheson, on the other hand, was far more misanthropic as a writer, which eradicated a great many barriers that prevented Bradbury from exploring true horror. But as was Bradbury's style, hope was always an eternal underlying theme in much of his works. As for Matheson, it was the classic hero's journey that provided much of the drive behind his stories. It was when Richard Matheson forced his heroes to confront true evil or the embodiment of that evil that the tales got really interesting. Whether it is lonely scientist Robert Neville trying to survive an apocalypse in *I Am Legend*, or William Shatner facing his demons on an airplane wing in the classic *Twilight Zone* episode "Nightmare at 20,000 Feet," Matheson always liked to put his main characters through Hell, as if he were curious to see what would happen and how it would turn out. But above all else, you cared about his characters and what happened to them. That's what made *I Am Legend*, *A Stir of Echoes*, *The Legend of Hell House*, and *What Dreams May Come* so engrossing, terrifying, and heartbreaking. His Boogeymen were formidable, terrifying creatures the likes of which had never been read, and there was never a guarantee that the hero would triumph.

To say Bradbury and Matheson were influential writers is a gross understatement. Stephen King, Peter Straub, and Clive Barker have always attested to this when asked about their influences, though Barker seems to have truly taken on Lovecraft's mantle as the writer of oddly detailed worlds more so than he has interpolated any of Matheson or Bradbury's influence. Both King and Straub go to great lengths to make the locations in their novels as alive as possible, much in the same way Bradbury did with Green Town, Illinois. Peter Straub created the quaint town of Milburn, which first appeared in his 1979 novel *Ghost Story* and would go on to make appearances in both *Koko* and *Floating Dragon*. King, in turn, would create not only Derry, but Castle Rock and Jerusalem's Lot, all small, devilish towns in his home state of Maine. Derry would appear in no less than six of his own books and became home to one of the greatest Boogeymen ever created. It is in Derry where Pennywise The Dancing Clown, the vile creature from *IT*, nestled in for the long haul before facing defeat hundreds of years after beginning a cyclical ritual of gruesome child murders. Pennywise reawakened everyone's fear of clowns and even made those who liked clowns before question why they enjoyed them in the first place. But Pennywise wasn't King's only, or best, boogeyman. Mr. Barlow from *'Salem's Lot*, Randall Flagg from *The Stand*, *Christine* and *Cujo* from their respective titular novels, Frank Dodd and Gregg Stillson from *The Dead Zone*, and Annie Wilkes from *Misery* are some of his greatest villains, not only because they are brutal and unforgiving; they work so well as characters because we see the weakness within them and are still terrified.

Peter Straub's greatest work, in my opinion, was his 1979 book, *Ghost Story*, which told the story of four old men haunted—literally—by a secret from their youth. As the ghostly Eva Galli takes her revenge, it's hard not to sympathize, not only with her quest for justice, but also for the men who made a terrible mistake in their youth and were tormented by it ever since. I actually prefer the film version of *Ghost Story* over the original novel; the somewhat tangled narratives and intersecting story lines are fleshed out better and there is a more steady focus on the main story of these four men and their atrocious crime. A close runner-up to *Ghost Story* would be *KOKO*, Straub's haunting tale of four Vietnam veterans who come together to find a serial killer who may or may not be a member of their old platoon. Also of note is his brilliant tale *Floating Dragon* about a mythical wraith who returns to the town of Hampstead, Connecticut, every thirty years to cause as much bloodshed and pain as possible. It is a hypnotically written, beautifully horrific novel that obviously influenced King to create the ever-returning Pennywise for *IT*.

As for Clive Barker? Who could forget the Cenobites of his brutal novella, *The Hellbound Heart*? They are Lovecraftian foes born of blood and fire, saints of pain and torture. They search out those seeking pleasure and offer it to them through the administration of indescribable pain. Using the fabled Lament Configuration puzzle box as a portal to the world of humans, they ensnare hedonist Frank Cotton, who thinks he is going to be visited by a bevy of demonic, lusty ladies. What he gets are the horribly scarred, sexless Cenobites, who dole out the same kind of punishing torture to everyone. But some see the torture as blissful and orgasmic, while others find the pain to be complete and absolute Hell. Either way, the Cenobites win. But Barker created an even better Boogeyman for his short story "The Forbidden," a character that would go on to become one of the most iconic in horror film history. Appearing in volume five of his popular *Books of Blood* series (published in the United States as *In The Flesh*), "The Forbidden" tells the tale of Helen, a university student who is doing her masters thesis on urban graffiti. She finds odd graffiti tags in the slums of Liverpool that tell of the legend of The Candyman, a Boogeyman who may or may not be responsible for a rash of murders in the slums. The film versions of both stories, *Hellraiser* and *Candyman*, became some of the most popular franchises in film history.

FILM AND TELEVISION

BOOGEYMEN WERE MADE for the movies and for television. The visual arts are so much of what makes a Boogeyman creepy that a well-made horror film or TV show can scar someone tremendously. For me, it was the 1970 TV movie *Don't Be Afraid of the Dark* that scared the bejeezus out of me and kept my feet from dangling over the side of the bed for the rest of my life. That movie, about a young woman tormented by little devilish creatures in an old dark house, still gives me the creeps.

I just shivered as I wrote that.

Sincerely.

The Boogeyman has played a role in film since the inception of motion pictures began in 1896 with Georges Méliès *House of The Devil* and 1897's *The Devil's Castle*. These two shorts are often regarded as being the first horror motion pictures ever produced. But the horror craze didn't get into full swing until 1910 with the Thomas Edison produced *Frankenstein*. Running only twelve minutes, the film is a very condensed version of the novel with spectacularly produced (for the time, that is) special effects. The year 1920 begat Roger Weine's *The Cabinet of Dr. Caligari*, which introduced us to Cesare, a black-clad somnambulist with a penchant for predicting dire futures at a carnival. This would be followed by Carl Boese's take on the Golem legend with *Der Golem*. Finally, in 1922, German auteur F. W. Murnau introduced us to his version of the Strigoi when Count Orlok made his appearance in the classic film *Nosferatu*. It is no mere coincidence that these films originated with artists who grew up with the folklore of Germany and France in their blood. Their visions of The Boogeyman were grotesque and terrifying, unrepentant and villainous, unlike the romanticized versions of Frankenstein's Monster, Dracula, and The Wolf Man that Hollywood created in the 1930s and 1940s. Films like *The Blob*, *The Monster That Challenged the World*, and *The Thing* would carry on the tradition of terrifying monsters, even as other filmmakers insisted on making silly ones such as *Attack of the Crab Monsters* and *The Killer Shrews*.

But the 1970s would reinvigorate the horror genre like no other decade in history, and The Boogeyman enjoyed a welcome return to true horror. While the early 1970s belonged to Satanic-driven films such as *The Exorcist* and *The Omen*, the latter half of the decade belonged to the Slashers. While few see little difference between the two genres, Tenebris is quick to point out that one genre is inspired by the Devil, while the others were directly influenced by him alone. John Carpenter used him as his jumping-off point for *Halloween*, a classic B horror movie that constantly refers to its antagonist, Michael Myers, as The Boogeyman, and with good reason. Michael is an unstoppable creature that cannot be reasoned with, much like The Boogeyman I met and the one you just read about. But in Tenebris's case, his speaking voice is much better. Of course, *Halloween* led to more Boogeymen, such as Jason Voorhees from the *Friday the 13th* series of films, and Freddy Krueger from *Wes Craven's A Nightmare on Elm Street* and its sequels. Jason, Freddy, and Michael are classic urban legends brought to the screen using every hook and turn that the classic fables offered. They were Boogeymen who punished kids for their transgressions, making them indistinguishable next to creatures like The Mare, Baba Yaga, and the Grylla.

The Boogeyman homages would become even clearer with the appearance of Bughuul in *Sinister*, who is portrayed as a Sumerian soul-eating demon who preys on children, in the demented world of *Silent Hill*, where the ominous Pyramid Head wields an enormous sword and stalks the foggy streets of a mythical American small town, and as a singing and dancing piece of stitched-together burlap known as Oogie Boogie in *Tim Burton's The Nightmare Before Christmas*. Films like *The Babadook*, *Adam Green's Hatchet*, and *Mama* also paid glorious tribute to the big guy under the bed (or in the closet.)

Tim Burton is perhaps the greatest advocate of The Boogeyman in that he embraces the dark and whimsical fables of his youth and perhaps even the exciting happenings that went on underneath his bed when he was a child. From his dark collection of early drawings and poems that led to *The Nightmare Before Christmas* and both incarnations of his classic *Frankenweenie*, Tim Burton has led the charge to bring The Boogeyman to the masses in nearly every film he's ever done. *Beetlejuice*, *Edward Scissorhands*, *Sweeney Todd*, *The Headless Horseman*, and even *Willy Wonka* have that Boogey-ish essence to them. Burton goes to great lengths to not only make them frightening, but endearing and lovable as well. Its no wonder that he's become godlike in Goth communities around the world.

But the true legends of The Boogeyman and his more ancient forms would not be forgotten, either. The new millennium gave rise to the rebirth of ogres, trolls, and even the nastier side of Santa. Tolkien's ogres, orcs, trolls, and goblins came out to play in both *The Lord of The Rings* and *The Hobbit* films. But while those films based their Boogeymen on fantasy fiction, 2010's Sweden incredible docu-drama *Trollhunter* and Finland's *Rare Exports: A Christmas Tale* brilliantly revived the legends of old Norse trolls and the once-almighty Santa Claus and his nasty little minions, the ever-helpful workshop elves. Even Michael Dougherty's 2015 Christmas fable *Krampus* managed to retain the playfulness and the horror of Christmas's most feared curmudgeon from the Austrian and German folktales of old.

Of course, the illustration of Boogeymen at work couldn't get any more vivid than Disney/Pixar's *Monster's Inc.* and its sequel/prequel, *Monsters University*. Centering on the Yeti-like polka-dotted James P. "Sully" Sullivan and cyclopian green globule Mike Wazowski, the films brilliantly shine a positive and hilarious light on the plight of professional "scarers" in an odd utopia filled with monsters who travel to human worlds via special doors, a place where the screams of children fuel their entire world. In the end, it is revealed that laughter is a stronger fuel, but it is an ending Tenebris hotly refutes as anti-fear propaganda. Go figure.

Then there are the films that overtly used The Boogeyman's name and reputation to every advantage possible, beginning with 1980's *The Boogeyman*, in which a haunted mirror was said to be possessed by the titular character. It was followed by *The Boogeyman II* in 1983, as well as the little-known creature feature *The Boogens* in 1981. It wasn't until 2005, with the release of Stephen Kay's *Boogeyman*, did the Thing in the closet get a more accurate portrayal as a young man returns to his childhood home to confront not only his childhood fears, but The Boogeyman himself. The mediocre success of this film ensured even more lackluster direct-to-video sequels, which came out in 2007 and 2008. Also tossed generously into the fray of Boogeyman-inspired films were 2003's *Darkness Falls* and 2013's *Heebie Jeebies*. None of them did well commercially and audiences pretty much abandoned them to die at the box office.

But not all of them were misses. In the midst of all the horror business came a set of films that accurately portrayed true Boogeymen in their natural habitat. Unfortunately, they were two films that were directed by a sort of Boogeyman in his own right. Victor Salva, a promising young director in the horror genre, was finishing up his first wide-release horror film, 1989's *Clownhouse* about a boy terrorized by a trio of psychotic clowns, when he was arrested, tried, and convicted of molesting his twelve-year-old star. Eleven years later, after serving his time in prison and exorcising the demons he had inside of him, Salva returned to the horror genre with the agonizingly terrifying *Jeepers Creepers* (2001.) With an antagonist known only as The Creeper, Victor Salva's monster preyed on those who had prime body parts he needed to make himself appear more human. The film was a welcome return to primal, guttural films that were actually scary and well made.

Television and motion pictures offered some of the best examples of Boogeymen in their natural habitat. Barnabas Collins was one of the first, a vampire in his very own soap opera called *Dark Shadows*. Created by Dan Curtis, the show revolved around the Collins family of Collinsport, Maine. It was a regular soap opera-type show, except there was a vampire, a few witches here and there, and a werewolf. And a few ghosts. Maybe a zombie. The point is there were no limits to *Dark Shadows*; Curtis pulled out all the stops and created a love-lorn *Twilight Zone* full of monsters to play with, and it worked pretty well. Curtis would go on to create even more Boogeymen for his show *Kolchak: The Night Stalker* and his most well known made-for-TV film, *Trilogy of Terror* (which featured Karen Black battling it out with the notorious Zuni fetish doll. Hint: it doesn't go well for Karen Black.)

Dan Curtis opened doors for people who'd grown tired of the same old *Twilight Zone* episodes. In the late 1960s and early 1970s, Hammer

Films out of England produced gory versions of *Frankenstein, Dracula, and The Wolf Man* to astounding success, both critical and commercial. As the tide turned toward a more exploitative Boogeyman, television churned out horror and fantasy shows like *Night Gallery, Tales of The Unexpected, The X-Files, Amazing Stories, Tales From the Crypt, Supernatural,* and *Grimm,* all of which use the age old tradition of fables and folklore to paint their dark tapestries of horrific drama. Even children shows got in on the act, treating us to thoroughly surreal (and often very funny) episodes of *R. L. Stine's Goosebumps, The Grim Adventures of Billy and Mandy,* and *Courage, the Cowardly Dog.* The trend of television nightmares continues to this day with *The Walking Dead, Hannibal,* and *Penny Dreadful,* though in the more recent cases, The Boogeyman tends to look and act more human than ever before.

Maybe that's what's scariest of all. The Boogeyman is us. He's not under the bed, he's in our head, counting fears and drinking tears, he licks his lips and waits to say, "Come out, come out, it's time to play."

APPENDIX II

DISSECTING THE DEMON

THE PHILOSOPHY OF NIGHTMARES

I'M USED TO people doubting me. With this rather unbelievable story of Tenebris, The Boogeyman, and his adventures, they will continue to doubt me. I've been blessed with a lot of friends in the paranormal field, but few of them are willing to go out on a limb and believe in a fantastic tale based on the blind faith of the storyteller. Paranormal nerds need facts and don't really give much credence to stories, legends, and myths. And while I'm hardly a scientist by any stretch of the imagination, I thought it was important to explore, at least in a decidedly generic form, the essence of nightmares and night terrors. This is a small, but no less earnest effort to examine the inner workings of terror, particularly the terror that comes in the dark when we're asleep.

I won't bore you with facts about why humans and other mammals need sleep; it should be fairly obvious that sleep brings about a recharging process, not only for our physiological needs, but also to maintain our psychological health. Disruptions in sleep, and particularly one brand of sleep psychosis that I want to focus on, are referred to by scientists as parasomnias. Simply put, parasomnias are episodes that occur during sleep that may cause an interruption but don't interfere with the quality of sleep. Some are good experiences as your brain shows you your deepest desires, answers your most enduring questions, or takes you to fantastic dream-scapes that you could never possibly see during waking life.

But there are other shows the brain likes to play at night: disturbing, frightening, and very realistic episodes of acute horror. These psychodramas can be so traumatic to children that, as adults, we can still relate every single detail of the nightmare with frightening clarity. What makes nightmares so traumatizing is that it seems like our brain is deliberately trying to destroy our psyche. What's even worse is that the brain is doing everything it can to make you helpless to its sick horror show. The brain, while the body sleeps, releases chemicals, like melatonin, that help keep you sleep, basically sedating and keeping you that way. Then, when you least expect it, the brain hits you with its latest show of the night. Hopefully, it'll be an escapade in a field with your high school sweetheart, or maybe a tryst with the celebrity of your choice. In the very least, you hope its not one of those "naked in school and late for finals" kinds of dreams. But sometimes, the brain likes to send you on the ultimate dark ride, a carnival ride of terror that uses every insecurity you've ever had in your entire life against you. And, man, the brain is flipping merciless sometimes.

With the standard nightmare, you might find yourself awake, heart racing, and your brow covered in sweat, combined with a deep reluctance to go back to sleep. With night terrors, however, the sufferer can begin screaming in their sleep, followed by frenzied races around the house. Someone under the influence of night terrors will literally do anything they can to physically avoid the terror the brain is showing them, but they don't understand what is happening. They can't escape because the horror is already inside them. But unlike nightmares, those who suffer night terrors likely won't remember what they dreamed or that they gave everyone else in the house quite a show at two in the morning.

Illnesses that generate high fevers, reactions to nervous system medications, and post-traumatic stress disorder are but a few of the causes of nightmares and night terrors, but there have also been theories that they can be inherited from parents. The landscape of nightmares and dreams is vast, and many of the caves within it are unexplored territories. Anytime a discovery is made in the science of dreams, a contradicting theory can arise just as quickly in the realm of nightmares.

Sleep paralysis is one of the newer classifications of sleep disorders, but it is not a new occurrence. This is the part of the nightmare where Tenebris comes in to play. In experiencing sleep paralysis, the sufferer undergoes the inability to move, speak, or react to things around them during that wonderfully alarming transition of going from deeply asleep to being wide awake. In that gray area between sleeping and waking, the body is weak and the sufferer finds it difficult to move, most likely because the chemicals transmitted from the brain to the body are still effectively anesthetizing it. Sleep paralysis is often accompanied by terrifying hallucinations (or by Tenebris, who is trying desperately to wrench fright out of you), making you believe that something is keeping you from moving, and let's face it: the idea that our brain is working against us while we sleep is infinitely more frightening than anything Tenebris could make up. We'd much rather believe that something outside of our body is restricting our movements. It leads us to believe that we are nothing but fleshy vehicles for the insidious brain to get around in, which is pretty terrifying, I must say.

But in truth, most of the time, our brains know what's best for us, even when its making us wet our beds with all the goofy stuff it makes us watch. The art of lucid dreaming can help one shape the features of their dreams, but it is an art that is difficult to master. At its essence, lucid dreaming is the art of knowing you are dreaming while still maintaining perfect sleep and manipulating the dream world to suit your own comfort levels, not the ones your brain thinks are good for you. For instance, if your brain wants to throw a buxom blonde in a pink bunny suit and clown makeup wielding a rusty chain saw at you, you can counter it by turning the buxom blonde bunny into a purple rabbit's foot key chain that you stuff in your pocket. But in doing so, are you ignoring the issues the brain wants you to face, issues you need to overcome in order to grow psychologically? There certainly are just as many detriments to lucid dreaming as there are benefits. Teaching it to those who suffer chronic, uninitiated nightmares has been proven to reduce the frequency of nightmares overall, but little research has been conducted focusing on the lack of psychological exploitation of traumatic baggage.

Nightmares, like dreams, are an essential component of sleep, for only during nightmares do we see the world of our insecurity for what it truly is: an unending sea of potential failure, and we get to see this potential failure as what-could-be instead of what-will-be. We see a possible future and are given the opportunity to change it in the real world by recognizing, fighting, and defeating our inner demons.

In fact, I say nightmares are more important than good dreams. Good dreams are the glossy photos of our favorite magazine. Nightmares are dirty pages torn from our favorite books that contain our favorite passages, and they just so happen to map out our entire psychological make-up. We're a dash of *Lord of the Flies*, a pinch of *Gone with the Wind*, a healthy dose of *The Hobbit*, and a sprinkling of *Alice in Wonderland*, all topped off (if we're lucky) with a liberal helping of *Fanny Hill* or *Lady Chatterley's Lover*. Our nightmares are the truest visions of our inner selves made brutally, painfully visible in our mind's eye in a way that is unfiltered and unrepentant. It is in the midst of a nightmare that we are the most honest we will ever be with ourselves.

ACKNOWLEDGMENTS

Extended, major thanks to Pete Schiffer and Schiffer Publishing; to my illustrious and venerable editor, Dinah Roseberry; to all my friends, family, and supporters: I love you all and no ruler can measure the thanks I have for your continued support; to the late Ray Bradbury, Richard Matheson, and Richard Laymon, Stephen King, Peter Straub, and Edward Levy for showing me the power darkness has on a printed page; and finally, To Tenebris, the one true Boogeyman, for taking a chance on me and allowing me to tell your tale. I hope I did okay by you.

BIBLIOGRAPHY

Asma, Stephen T. *On Monsters: An Unnatural History of Our Worst Fears.* New York: Oxford University Press; Reprint edition, 2011.

Emden, Rabbi Jacob. *Megilat Sefer: The Autobiography of Rabbi Jacob Emden.* Originally published in 1748. New English translation by Sidney B. and Meir H. Wise. Republished February 2016 by Shaftek Enterprises, LLC.

Greer, John Michael. *Monsters: An Investigator's Guide to Magical Beings.* Minnesota: Llewellyn Publications, 2001.

Grimm, Jacob. *Grimm's Teutonic Mythology.* Online PDF translation published via archive.spectator.co.uk.

Hartmann, Dr. Ernest. *The Nightmare: The Psychology and Biology of Terrifying Dreams.* Basic Books, 1986.

Hill, Dr. Ann. *What To Do When Dreams Go Bad: A Practical Guide To Nightmares.* Serpentine Music & Media, 2009.

Hollis, E. Crossman. "Beowulf" review. ExodusBooks.com.

Hutton, Ronald. *The Triumph of the Moon: A History of Modern Pagan Witchcraft.* New York: Oxford University Press, 2001.

Keel, John A. *The Mothman Prophecies.* New York: Saturday Review Press and E. P. Dutton, 1975.

Melhorn, Gary. *The Esoteric Codex: Shapeshifters.* Originally published March 2015. Public Domain. Research copy found on PDF via LuLu.com.

Poole, W. Scott. *Monsters in America: Our Historical Obsession with the Hideous and the Haunting.* Texas: Baylor University Press, 2014.

Shelley, Mary Wollstonecraft. *Frankenstein, or The Modern Prometheus — The 1818 Uncensored Edition.* Wisehouse Publications, 2015

Steiger, Brad. *Real Monsters, Gruesome Critters, and Beasts from the Darkside.* Michigan: Visible Ink Press, 2010.

Warner, Marina. *No Go The Bogeyman: Scaring, Lulling, And Making Mock.* Farrar, Straus and Giroux, February 16, 1999.

Wojcik, Jonathon. "7 Horrific Boogeymen Used To Scare Kids Around The World." Cracked.com, October 29, 2009.

MUCH OF MY RESEARCH ENTAILED FINDING INFORMATION ON THE FOLLOWING WEBSITES:

americanfolklore.net
archive.org
bartleby.com
creepypasta.com
dagonbytes.com
dailymail.co.uk
europeisnotdead.com
exodusbooks.com

huffingtonpost.com
indianabigfootreports.com
ingebretsens.com
mysteriousbritain.co.uk
native-languages.org
nytimes.com
people.com
somethingawful.com

thedemoniacal.blogspot.com
vikinganswerlady.com
viralnova.com
vrsidor.se
whitedragon.org.uk
wikiart.com

"EVERYTHING YOU WANT, NEED, AND
DESIRE LIES ON THE OTHER SIDE OF FEAR.
WILL YOU CHALLENGE THE DARK, OR
WILL IT CHALLENGE YOU?"

—Tenebris, The Boogeyman. (*Photo by author.*)